If you plan for a decade, plant trees,
If you plan for a century, nurture children.

(Origin unknown)

Text copyright © Gill Dallow 2002
Appendix 1 copyright © Becky Holland 2002

The author asserts the moral right
to be identified as the author of this work

Published by
The Bible Reading Fellowship
First Floor, Elsfield Hall
15–17 Elsfield Way, Oxford OX2 8FG
ISBN 1 84101 140 1
First published 2002
10 9 8 7 6 5 4 3 2 1 0
All rights reserved

Acknowledgments
Unless otherwise stated, scripture quotations are from the *Contemporary English Version*
© American Bible Society 1991, 1992, 1995. Used by permission/Anglicizations
© British and Foreign Bible Society 1997.

Scripture quotations taken from the *Holy Bible, New International Version*, copyright
© 1973, 1978, 1984 by International Bible Society. Used by permission of Hodder &
Stoughton Limited. All rights reserved. 'NIV' is a registered trademark of International
Bible Society, UK trademark number 1448790.

Scriptures quoted from the Good News Bible published by The Bible
Societies/HarperCollins Publishers Ltd, UK © American Bible Society 1966, 1971, 1976,
1992, used with permission.

Excerpts from 'The Formative Nature of Liturgy: Cultic Life and the Initiation of
Children' by John H. Westerhoff III published in *Issues in the Christian Initiation of
Children: Catechesis and Liturgy*, © 1989 Archdiocese of Chicago: Liturgy Training
Publications, 1800 N. Hermitage Ave. Chicago Il. 60622. orders@ltp.org. All rights
reserved. Used with permission.

A catalogue record for this book is available from the British Library

Printed and bound in Great Britain by
Omnia Books Limited, Glasgow

Touching the Future

A handbook for church-based children's leaders

GILL DALLOW

For my husband Roger Dallow who, though he died at the age of 28, by his leadership and vision for children and young people's work, inspired me to become a teacher and trainer and thereby to be able to touch the future.

For the children in my life with whom I am privileged to help touch the future—my nieces and nephews, Ceri, Lynne, Alison, James, Andrew, Caroline, William and Sarah; and my godchildren, Susan, Victoria, Emma, Stephen, Bethany... and not forgetting the children in my parish of St Giles Barlestone in the diocese of Leicester.

Acknowledgments

I am grateful to the many friends and colleagues I have worked with over the years who have had a share in the creation of this training handbook. Especially crucial have been Paul Butler, Kathryn Copsey, Peter Graystone, Christine Wright, Alan Price, David and Pauline Pearson, all of whom worked with me at London Bible College in setting up one of the earliest children's ministry courses in the UK as part of the degree of Bachelor of Theology. We all had one thing in common—a pioneering spirit and vision to provide competent and 'cutting edge' children's and young people's leaders.

Second, I would like to thank those in the diocese of Leicester who have encouraged yet another pioneering venture in the establishing of a diocesan-accredited advisers' training course for children and young people, 'Touching the Future'. The content of this training manual forms a large part of the curriculum. My thanks especially to John and Jane Leonard and Betty Jordan for their practical support in implementing this course.

Finally, my thanks to the Bishop of Leicester, the Rt Revd Tim Stevens, and the Archdeacon of Loughborough, the Venerable Ian Stanes; also to the clergy and leaders in the diocese of Leicester for their part in supporting and developing ministry among children and young people and thereby helping to 'touch the future'.

Contents

Foreword 7

Introduction: Training the new generation 8

Section 1: Knowing our theological roots 17
Chapter 1: Children from the Old Testament perspective..............18
Chapter 2: Children from Jesus' perspective....................................33
Chapter 3: Children in the early Christian community 44

Section 2: How children grow 52
Chapter 4: Whatever happened to childhood? 53
Chapter 5: Child development 56
Chapter 6: The child's social world 59
Chapter 7: How children think...71
Chapter 8: Spirituality and faith development 78

Section 3: Leading children into worship 93
Chapter 9: Belonging to a worshipping community........................94
Chapter 10: Worship in the home...104
Chapter 11: All-age worship 113
Chapter 12: Children and spiritual gifts 121
Chapter 13: Using the Bible with children 129
Chapter 14: Leading children into prayer 139

Section 4: Strategies for action...147
Chapter 15: Growing a group..148
Chapter 16: A strategy for learning..169
Chapter 17: Reaching children on the fringe 182

Appendices

Appendix One: Setting up a midweek club 194
Appendix Two: Evaluation form 213
Appendix Three: Commissioning service 215
Appendix Four: Towards a Charter for Children
                             in the Church (URC) 217

Bibliography 219

Agencies working with children and young people 228

Subject index 237

Scripture index 239

Foreword

Of all the tasks facing the contemporary Church, the evangelization of children is the most urgent. It simply cannot wait. As generations grow up who have never heard the gospel of Jesus Christ, except in passing, the need for effective proclamation of the good news becomes ever more pressing. The fact that over 50 per cent of Anglican parishes now have no children's or youth work tells the story. Without action, the Church of tomorrow will be in danger of withering on the demographic vine.

But what to do? Faced with the realities of a heavily secularized culture, many have all but given up in despair. Fortunately, Gill Dallow has not. As a teacher at London Bible College, Gill was responsible for the first children's ministry course in the UK. For the last four years she has worked this out in practice as the vicar of a Leicestershire parish that has seen rapid growth in its children's work. And on top of this, she has pioneered a diocesan-wide course designed to train advisers in the Church's ministry to children and young people. Gill is no mere theorist but a practitioner of the first order.

In *Touching the Future*, therefore, we are privileged in having the insights, experience and reflection of a ministry that is grounded in a love for children and a love for Christ. This has given Gill's writing a rare combination of educational insight, theological reflection and practical application. As readers will quickly discover, each chapter is packed with gems. We can be confident that she speaks with well-earned authority.

There are few books about which I would say, 'Sell your shirt to get it!' This is one of them.

Revd Dr Francis Bridger
Principal, Trinity College, Bristol, and author of Children Finding Faith

I highly commend the vision and energy reflected in this training manual, already successfully field-tested in the Diocese of Leicester. My hope is that it will be an inspiration and a significant guide for many leaders who, in this greatly under-resourced area of church life, through their ministry and training of children and young people, 'touch the future'.

+ *Tim Leicester*

Introduction

TRAINING THE NEW GENERATION

My friends, I beg you to listen as I teach. I will give instruction and explain the mystery of what happened long ago. These are things we learnt from our ancestors, and we will tell them to the next generation. We won't keep secret the glorious deeds and the mighty miracles of the Lord. God gave his law to Jacob's descendants, the people of Israel. And he told our ancestors to teach their children, so that each new generation would know his Law and tell it to the next.
PSALM 78:1–6

Everyone who has the privilege to nurture and reach out to children, whether as a parent, a teacher, a church leader or children's leader, has the privilege to 'touch the future', for it is their generation who will take God's Church forward into the future. If we believe this, before us is a vital agenda for our church leadership to address at this time.

Using this book

Too often, training for children's ministry is the 'Cinderella' of the church. A lack of training has resulted in poor practice at church level and an inadequate knowledge on the part of church leaders as to the needs of those working with children. This is a training handbook to suit all levels. It is not aimed at any particular age group as it covers general principles for church-based leaders working with children and young people across the age range. The foundational material was originally devised and field-tested as part of the Bachelor of Theology Degree course in my capacity as Director of Training at London Bible College. Subsequently, it has been used for *Touching the Future*, an authorized children's and young people's training course in Leicester Diocese. This course was set up in 2001 to train volunteers as recognized children's and young people's advisers, similar to the Anglican ministries of Lay Reader, Evangelist and Pastoral Assistant.

This handbook has been designed for individual use as well as to complement such training courses. It is important to note that while this manual provides a comprehensive training resource for church-based children's and young people's leaders, it is not exhaustive. There is obviously more to explore and develop in this field. As I have tried to cover much ground, it has not been possible to include such matters as initiation rites and the admission of the baptized to Holy Communion. Similarly, the pastoral care of children and child protection issues have not been addressed in depth within the main body of the text, although suggestions for resource material are included in the final appendix.

To obtain maximum benefit from this training resource, it is highly recommended that readers develop their own training journal, using the reflection and evaluation process outlined below.

Unless otherwise stated, the version of the Bible used is the CEV (Contemporary English Version), a very helpful translation to be used with children themselves.

Reflection process

The following guidelines might be helpful in reflecting on the material in each chapter.

Before reading a chapter
What questions are in your mind and what are you hoping to get out of this chapter?

While reading the material
Make a note of any points significant for your situation. What new questions have arisen for you from this chapter?

At the end of the chapter
How has your thinking been changed? What action will you take to put into practice this new thinking?

The shape of the new generation

This section is designed to give an overview of some changes experienced within contemporary culture that shape the new generation of children in our churches today. By the end of this section we will:
- Be able to share something of our children's life experience from their point of view.
- Have a better understanding of the children we work with and the factors that influence them.

Have a conversation with two children, one under and one over seven years of age, with a view to discovering something about their experience of the world they live in. Ask them about the things they like doing, the music they play, clothes they wear, food they eat, their friends, their families and their school life. What about their fears? Does God mean anything to them? Do they have any contact with church?

In the light of that conversation, what changes do you think have taken place since your childhood? How does this affect your work with children and your understanding of the shape of the new generation? Now read on.

The new generation is different

We know this to be true: the children of the new generation are different! They dress differently; they sound and look different. They behave differently. They have an insatiable appetite for junk food, junk films, junk ideas and junk culture. Today's children are the first generation to grow up with AIDS and environmental catastrophes. They are living in a society in which everything is done for profit. In today's world, politics divide and disempower groups of people—especially themselves as children and young people and their families. They live in a society that relies for its survival on major technological advances and the changes such advances bring. The new generation is the inheritor of so-called 'benefits', and the silent victim of a bewildering speed of change. Does this change mean that our society expects more of the young?

REFLECTION

Think of the way education has been reshaped to produce higher achievers. What is our view of pupil progress? What do you think about assessment schemes to assist the planning of children's education and the measurement of their future education achievement? A piece in *The Sunday Times* in April 2000 made this observation: 'Spare the test and fail the child. The testing of children as young as seven may seem hard but it is by far the best way of raising standards.'

Do you agree?

The new generation lives in an electronic fish bowl

Children today are surrounded by an electronic world of virtual reality. Having already mastered laptops, the Internet, CD-ROMs, DVDs, faxes, modems, PlayStations and so on, they have a tremendous ability to process lots of information at once. They can play video games and talk on the phone at the same time. They can listen to their portable CDs and do their homework. Yes, the new generation has a complex experience of life. Today's children pick up a confused code of ethics, for what applies to one situation is so different from the next one.

What shapes children's thinking? Consider the concept of computer games. Often winning is the main concern; the world reduced to 'them against you'. To kill a screen character is to win a game. To survive (win) a video game requires the player to become a ruthless oppressor. Life for many children of this new generation has become a series of individualistic acts. The sense of living in community is lost. For example, the individual watches the programme, plays the game, manipulates the characters and constructs his or her own reality. The options offered are made by an anonymous programme designer. It is no longer possible for this new generation to make their own or communal options for choice. Such technology offers them a tremendous knowledge base as well as opportunities to explore the world through technology. But they are denied both the necessary community and sufficient opportunities to develop as moral and ethical people whose beliefs, values and ethics are not open to investigation or evaluation.

The new generation is dominated by image

Consider the following piece from the *Church of England Newspaper* in March 2000:

Today's children are spending more time watching TV or playing computer games than exercising. A study for Sport England of 3,000 children between ages 5 and 16 found that on average they spend 7.5 hours on sport or exercise compared with 11.4 hours watching TV or videos and 4.4 hours playing computer games. Only 11 per cent of children aged between 6 and 8 take part in the recommended minimum of two hours exercise weekly.

Consider how family life is seen on TV, not only in the soaps but also in a wide range of programmes. What effect might these images have on children and their own relationships within their own families?

Think about the impact of advertising for the latest PlayStation, not to mention icon role models, pop stars and so on:

Brash, brutal, and bigger than live football—wrestlers have become the role model for many youngsters in Britain. Should we be worried?
THE SUNDAY TIMES, 14 MAY 2000

Disney magics up girl rival to Harry Potter.
THE SUNDAY TIMES, 21 MAY 2000

REFLECTION

Take a look at a range of magazines aimed at different age groups. What message do they convey about lifestyles and family relationships? Take a look at the type of music on offer to our young generation. What do the lyrics tell us about our new generation? Listen to the different expressions, sometimes passionate, sometimes angry, sometimes rebellious and sometimes reflecting a real hunger for spiritual truth. How does this help us to understand the children we work with? How can we help children to control the media rather than being controlled by it? How can we provide help for children in discerning what is good?

The new generation lives for today

There are no longer jobs for life. Our young people will probably have a succession of jobs rather than a career. For many, the attitude today is: 'Work is what you do so that you can have a life'. Many young people growing up in today's world will prioritize relationships above work.

The new generation is globally aware

More than any other generation in the history of the human race so far, the new generation has access to what is going on across the world. The formal and informal effects of global education are seen in the way children address the issues about which they become concerned, and their awareness of other countries and cultures—perhaps to the detriment of their knowledge about their own country and culture. Young people are concerned about human rights issues and want to find ways to help children in need. Their own awareness of these issues means that they can find it difficult to understand why adults seem to know less than they do and perhaps appear so apathetic about global issues.

The new generation sees 'family' as a contradiction in terms

The word 'family' has come to mean anything in terms of human relationships and nothing in particular. Almost half of our children will experience their parents' separation and divorce, bringing an inevitable restructuring of their family. Fewer than half of children in today's society live with two biological parents throughout their childhood. For some children, family restructure means gaining 'new' parents who will attempt to influence their lives, gaining additional grandparents or losing a specific pair of parents.

The increase in two-job families has given rise to the 'latchkey' generation. In some cases, such children show anxiety about their personal identity and security in their family. Many children become the victims of the adults' poor-quality relationships and inability to cope with life. In spite of much talk in society about the problems of 'street kids', very little has been done to deal with root causes, most of which arise from dysfunctional families. On the other hand, many children are experiencing the benefits of an extended family, with several adults to whom they can relate.

The new generation is deprived

The Sunday Times on 23 April 2000 makes an observation: 'Once upon a time childhood was made of magic.'

Today many children have their childhood ruthlessly snatched away from them. Abuse and violence are rampant around the world. The United Nations description of a normal childhood has become a hollow mockery to millions:

The children of the world are innocent, vulnerable and dependent. They are also curious, active and full of hope. Their time should be one of joy and peace, of playing, learning and growing. Their future should be shaped in harmony and cooperation. Their lives should mature as they broaden their perspectives and gain new experiences.

This glimpse of the ideal image of childhood highlights the tragedy that millions of children live in difficult circumstances. It reveals the depth of loss that children experience when they are deprived of a normal, healthy childhood. Children in much of the world are no longer provided with a living environment conducive to their happiness, growth and development. Traditionally, people assume that adult members of society will protect children. However, in many societies, children as young as three years old must now be taught to protect themselves from violence and abuse. More children than ever are being forced to learn two extremely painful lessons: first of all, the world is no longer a safe place in which to live; and second, adults cannot always be trusted. What an indictment!

Dorothy Law Nolte has stated this principle in her well-known assertions in *Children Learn What They Live* (American Institute of Family Relations).

- If a child lives with criticism, he learns to condemn
- If a child lives with hostility, he learns to fight
- If a child lives with ridicule, he learns to be shy
- If a child lives with shame, he learns to feel guilty
- If a child lives with tolerance, he learns to be patient
- If a child lives with encouragement, he learns confidence
- If a child lives with praise, he learns to appreciate
- If a child lives with fairness, he learns justice
- If a child lives with security, he learns to have faith
- If a child lives with approval, he learns to like himself
- If a child lives with acceptance and friendship, he learns to find love in this world

The new generation: a blind spot in Christian ministry

Childhood and early teens, sometimes described as the '4–14 window', are often the years when young people make a faith commitment for themselves.

The deluge of training materials and publications over the past thirty years on the development of ministry with this new generation have examined strategies and models of learning and faith development. There has been only a little in-depth research relating to a theology of childhood. But the work that has been done has highlighted some crucial issues.

The General Synod of the Church of England's report *Children in the Way* (1988) examined the position of the young as being equal partners in the journey of faith. The sobering statistics in another report, *All God's Children?* (1991), showed that 87 per cent of children in this country have no contact with any Christian church. On a global scale, MARC estimates that 85 per cent of young people—1.4 billion of the total 1.8 billion—are growing up in non-Christian settings.

Unfinished Business (1995), a report by the CCBI (The Consultative Group on Ministry among Children), identified changes in Western family life that radically affect the traditional pattern of worship and learning. Change is inherent in the growth of a new generation but the churches' ways of addressing the former gentler pace of change is no longer sufficient.

A further General Synod Report, *Youth A Part* (1996), looking at issues in the Church of England among the new generation, considered the issue of how church and young people work in partnership as we move forward into the future.

Exploring biblical teaching on the new generation is no mere academic exercise. We must rise to the challenge of fresh biblical reflection. Otherwise, we are without the theological underpinning that will guide us and give us the tools we need.

Summary

1 We need to accept that, for the new generation, the present is not merely preparation for life: real life is now.
2 Jesus' own approach to children teaches us that we ought never to instruct our children on the basis of their future worth.
3 We need to affirm our advocacy for this generation.
4 We need to be relevant to their situation.
5 We need to honour their social, spiritual and pastoral needs.

Further action

In your church's life and activities, what improvements need to be made, if any, to give your children a safe, happy and loving community? How will you try to share something of life from your children's experience? How will you help your church to rethink its attitude to the new generation?

SECTION ONE

Knowing our theological roots

Too often in our training as children's leaders we see the importance of gaining practical skills but fail to appreciate the need to grasp the biblical basis of why we should be involved in children's ministry. The purpose of this section is to explore some of the biblical perspectives relating to children and childhood and to assess how this information can shape the strategies and attitudes that need to be adopted in children's ministry today.

This section has three chapters. Chapter 1 examines the biblical perspective from the Old Testament, chapter 2 explores what Jesus thought of children and chapter 3 considers children through the eyes of the first Christian community.

Chapter 1

CHILDREN FROM THE
OLD TESTAMENT PERSPECTIVE

The material in this chapter is a preparation for the following chapters in which we look at childhood and children through the eyes of the New Testament, a viewpoint radically altered by the coming of Christ, with life no longer under law but redeemed by grace (see Galatians 3:23–25).

If we want to have some understanding of perspectives on childhood in the Old Testament, we must leave behind our modern Western culture and enter a very different world. Let us consider what the Old Testament meant by childhood. H.W. Wolff, in his *Anthropology of the Old Testament*, says that, according to the Old Testament, childhood can be described as a stage of life different from that of youth and maturity.

REFLECTION

Look up the following passages. How do they describe childhood as a distinctive stage of life?

CHILDREN

Infants: Deuteronomy 32:29
Children: Psalm 148:12

YOUTH

Deuteronomy 32:25
Ezekiel 9:6
Psalm 148:12

Belonging in the covenant community

To capture what it meant to belong to a community, we need to move away in our thinking from our Western individualistic perspective to the more oriental, community-centred outlook that described the ancient Hebrew people. Everyone was seen as part of such a community at different levels:
- The extended family: this included blood relatives, children, servants and so on.
- The clan: every family was part of a larger grouping.
- The tribe: several clans made up each tribe, and the tribes together constituted the nation of Israel.

The importance attached to this ordered community is well illustrated by the genealogies and lists of names and tribes we find in the Old Testament. Look at 1 Chronicles 1—9 and note how people are described. This is reminiscent of Gideon in Judges 6:15, who places himself in the context of his family, clan and tribe: 'My clan is the weakest one in Manasseh, and everyone else in my family is more important than I am.' Consider other examples: Saul in 1 Samuel 9:17–21; and Jeremiah in Jeremiah 1:1.

The importance of the community was evident. People gained their identity from knowing to which people they belonged. They were individuals within their community rather than apart from it or over against it. A strong link of solidarity within the community of God runs through both the Old and New Testaments. Children belong to that people. The picture of the child that emerges is of a group member rather than as an individual in his or her own right. Children were not seen as making any contribution to the community until they reached the age of knowing the law, that of twelve or thirteen years old.

Think of your family background and how you relate to any children within that structure. How does the family structure today compare with that of the Old Testament? What are the implications for children in our own community?

To answer this question, we need to understand how the Old Testament community saw itself in relation to God. The relationship between God and his people was that of a covenantal relationship. A covenant was a two-way agreement between two parties. When God made his covenant with Abraham, he did so saying, 'I will always keep the promise I have made to you and your descendants, because I am your God and their God... Abraham, you and all future members of your family must promise to obey me' (Genesis 17:7, 9). This set Israel apart from all the nations on the face of the earth and, in order to make that separation viable, God gave them their own land and pledged it to them for ever.

Now read Exodus 20. Here we see a national covenant and the giving of the law at Sinai. In the light of this special relationship, there always had to be Israelites to occupy the land and to worship God as the covenant people. Some essential tasks had to be done to ensure that this happened, and the implications in the covenant community were that children would be essential to fulfil those tasks.

Task one: fulfilling the creation command

The first command of God to human beings was, 'Have a lot of children!' (Genesis 1:28). The concept that the image of God in human beings was linked to the blessings of fruitfulness stood in marked contrast to the pagan fertility cults in which human beings tried to persuade the gods to allow fruitfulness. The command was given to the whole of humanity but adopted within the covenant relationship between God and Israel.

To produce a large family was seen to be a fulfilling of God's covenant with his people, and the birth of children was regarded as a result of God's blessing (Genesis 1:28; 12:2).

Look up the following references to see how vitally important children were in this regard:

Hagar: Genesis 16:7–11
Rebekah: Genesis 24:60
Isaac: Genesis 26:4
Ruth: Ruth 4:11–12

Being blessed with children was a task as well as a gift. To what extent would you say your work with children reflects these aspects?

Task two: continuing the family name

Children were valued for their potential as future adult members of the covenant community (boys) and as guardians of the family and bearers of the next generation (girls). Lack of belief in an afterlife (Psalm 88:3–9) meant that a man's hope of living on after death lay chiefly with the children to whom he passed his name. The whole of the man's personality was summed up in his name. Where a man's name lived on, there he lived on. The desperate measures resorted to by the daughters of Lot show how deep this desire went (Genesis 19:30–38).

It was vital to continue the family line and to have someone to inherit the property—hence the importance of sons who could continue the family line and fortune and preserve the family name. The concern that there must always be Israelites to occupy the land and to worship God as the covenant people had nothing to do with gender issues in contemporary thinking, but with the need to continue the family name. This would explain, for example, why Hannah prayed specifically for a son (1 Samuel 1:11).

The birth of a son was celebrated as the event that saved the family name. When children were born, the parents would rejoice not only in seeing new life but also in receiving a token of God's blessing. Note Eve's response in Genesis 4:1 to the birth of her firstborn, 'I'll name him Cain, because I got him with the help of the Lord'. To be without children was not just a sorrow but also a spiritual problem. If there were no children, there would be no continuation of the people of God. The law of Levirate marriage (Deuteronomy 25:5–10) provided for a kinsman to marry a childless widow and raise children to perpetuate the dead husband's family, 'to carry on his name' (v. 6). This partly explains the marriage of Boaz and Ruth in Ruth 4.

Names and a sense of identity were seen as important in the community of God. The whole of a person's personality was bound up in their name. Think about the children you know. How many of their names do you know? How do they know they belong to your group?

Task three: maintaining the covenant with God

There were two significant ways in which the covenant with God was maintained—first of all, through circumcision, by which a male Israelite was regarded as a member of the covenant community. God first ordered circumcision as a sign of the covenant he had made with Abraham: 'As the sign that you are keeping this promise, you must circumcise every man and boy in your family' (Genesis 17:10–11).

The covenant was impressed in the flesh of the newborn son in his organ of reproduction, as a sign that he was entering the covenant relationship which he would eventually pass on to his own children. Although females were not given any physically distinguishing mark of the covenant, God's promises were to them as well: the covenant to Abraham was with all his seed, not just with male descendants (Genesis 12:1–3; 15:5). Israelites were commanded to circumcise not only their children but also their servants, both native and foreign (Genesis 17:12–13). Only circumcised foreigners who were servants or resident aliens could share in the Passover, the feast of the Israelite community (Exodus 12:43). To be uncircumcised was to be outside the covenant. Any Israelite who failed in this respect was a covenant-breaker (Genesis 17:14); he could not be one of God's people and was put to death. This is why God threatened Moses with death if he failed to circumcise his son before returning to the people (Exodus 4:24–26).

The second way in which the covenant with God was maintained was through the consecration of the firstborn. The importance of children was further emphasized by the consecration of the firstborn to God, a requirement that was set in place from the time of the first Passover (Exodus 13:2). Children represented the whole nation, and the firstborn's right to a double portion of the father's estate balanced this responsibility (Deuteronomy 21:16–17). The consecration of the firstborn was also a declaration of the continuity and permanence of Israel's relationship with God. In laying special claim to the firstborn in each family, God was in effect laying claim to the succeeding generations as his own. Just as the birth of the first son ensured the all-important continuation of that family into the succeeding generation, so

God's claim to that son as symbolic of the next generation ensured the continuation of God's relationship with Israel into that generation also. Israel belonged to God 'from generation to generation'.

The question of sterility needs to be considered. Not all parents could bear children. With such an emphasis on children being a blessing and a gift, it is not surprising to find that sterility was considered a trial, a punishment from God or a disgrace.

Read the following passages:

Genesis 16:2   Genesis 30:1–9
Genesis 20:18   1 Samuel 1:5

What do they tell us about attitudes to sterility? Note how Sarah, Rachel and Leah tried to clear themselves by adopting the children that their maids bore to their husbands. How different is the Christian view of being unable to have children today? To what extent do we still see this as a curse from God?

Protection in the covenant community

The need for physical protection

From the outset, children were regarded as belonging to God's people within the covenant and were therefore seen as belonging to God himself. The Bible notes the weakness and vulnerability of children and hence their need of care. This vulnerability and weakness is seen most starkly in the situation of the fatherless. Alongside the widows and aliens, they are often referred to as poor and needy. Since they had lost their parents, they needed someone to provide them with food and so on. Children are seen in many ways to be in need of the protection of their parents and the community.

Read the following passages:

Exodus 22:21–24   Isaiah 1:17
Deuteronomy 10:18 Hosea 14:3

What do these passages tell us about the responsibility of the wider community to which children belonged?

The need for moral protection

Children were seen as full persons made in God's image, and so they could be caught up in human sinfulness just like any other person. The Bible also acknowledges that infants do not know right from wrong (Deuteronomy 1:39; Isaiah 7:14–16). They need to be helped to gain and develop a certain amount of knowledge before they are able to make their own moral choices.

Children are seen in many ways to be in need of the protection of their parents and the community. Protection of children was very much tied up with the concept that the Israelite father owned his children. He might sell them into slavery (Exodus 21:7). They might be seized by his creditors in lieu of repay-ment (2 Kings 4:1; Isaiah 50:1) or even offered as hostages (Genesis 42:37), and the father who failed to maintain discipline over his children was held responsible for their behaviour and shared in their punishment. To illustrate this point, look at the example of Eli's sons, who were guilty of bringing the worship of God into disrepute (1 Samuel 2:12—3:18).

However, while children were entirely subject to the authority of the father as head of the household and counted legally as his property, the practical effects of children's status as property were limited. There were only two legitimate grounds for a father to 'realize' the economic value of his children: first, if they sustained 'damage' or 'devaluation' (as in the cases of premature birth or miscarriage and the abuse of a virgin daughter); and second, if financial extremity forced him to sell their services as slaves or as pledges.

Children could not be used judicially as a means of punishing their fathers; nor could they be made to suffer judicially along with him for offences of which he alone was guilty.

Children may have had an economic value in some circumstances, but they retained basic human rights as persons. It would seem that there was a much greater concern in the Old Testament with the responsibility of the father for his children than with his rights over them.

For further research

Find out about some of the current legislation (for example, *The Children Act* 1989) which is designed to protect the child in today's society. How does the law do this? Look carefully, too, at the question of children's rights. You could also contact The National Children's Network, PO Box 179, Pocklington, YO42 2ZN; Telephone 0797 185 7271.

Worship in the covenant community

The theological significance of children in the continuance of God's relationship with Israel meant that children were involved in the worship life of the community. Little is said about the child's individual relationship with God, though it is acknowledged that children are able to experience God, worship and serve him.

Consider the following references as examples of this point.

Psalm 8:2: 'With praises from children and from tiny infants…'. Jesus acknowledged the fact that children can worship God when, having cleared out the temple, children in the temple area began to shout out 'praises to the Son of David'. Jesus accepted this praise from the children in response to the Pharisees' indignation and replied, 'Don't you know that the Scriptures say, "Children and infants will sing praises"?' (Matthew 21:12–16).

Psalm 148:11–12: 'Every king and every ruler, all nations on earth, every man and every woman, young people and old, come, praise the Lord!' At first glance, children appear to be at the bottom of the praise list, but this is not the case. The psalm calls upon all aspects of creation to salute the king, and the sequence of praise is significant. Verses 1–4 begin at the pinnacle, with the highest heavens, and then in descending order the praise is passed on to the earth (v. 7). From verse 8, the praise continues in ascending order, from the oceans to the kings of the earth. Finally, at the pinnacle of praise are 'the children too' (v. 12, GNB).

1 Samuel 1—3: Hannah laments her childlessness and receives Eli's assurance that the God of Israel will grant her heart's desire. A child is born and is named Samuel because 'she had asked the Lord for him' (1:20). The act of setting Samuel apart for the Lord reveals in a remarkable way the heights of a child's experience and service to God. In 1 Samuel 1:21–28, he is brought to the house of the Lord at Shiloh and given to the Lord 'for as long as he lives'. The story leaves no doubt about the Lord's acceptance of him. Samuel 'worshipped the Lord there' (v. 28, NIV) without any questions asked or doubts expressed. Samuel 'served the Lord' and his service was accepted (1 Samuel 2:18), and the end of 2:21 shows that Samuel 'grew up at the Lord's house' as an ongoing experience. 1 Samuel 2:26 states, 'Each day the Lord and his people liked Samuel more and more', indicating a close relationship with God. Then, 1 Samuel 3:1–18 describes how Samuel was called upon and spoken to by God and entrusted with an important revelation, which the aged Eli was not in a position to receive. Samuel's communication with God was such that he could be entrusted with an important mission. Finally, in 1 Samuel 3:19–21, we see that Samuel was constantly close to God.

Ecclesiastes 12:1: 'Keep your Creator in mind while you are young! In years to come, you will be burdened down with troubles and say, "I don't enjoy life any more."' The Preacher stressed that religious experience was not the preserve of adults but that youth had a special relationship with God.

Since children belonged to God's people, they were expected to celebrate as part of God's people and hence were regarded as an integral part of the worshipping community. In his book *A Theology of Children's Ministry*, L.O. Richards gives some suggestions as to how that integration could have taken place.

Regular festivals

The pattern of festivals and repeated cycle of weeks and years shaped the faith of the community, affirming again and again who the covenant people were and their relationship to their covenant God as creator and redeemer. Repeated recurring events within the year helped children to appreciate their roots as they relived the experiences of the past with all ages. Examples of such festivals are the Passover and the feast of Tabernacles (Exodus 12:25–27; Leviticus 23:34).

Religious institutions

Religious institutions communicated the faith of the community to its members. For example, worship was the central institution, focused on the Tabernacle, and its sacrifices, priestly service and even the architectural design of the Tabernacle were rich in symbolism. The use of symbol was an important means of introducing children into the worship of Israel. Familiar symbols would remain with them as they grew older, and would take on ever-deepening meaning as children grew in their understanding of their faith.

Visual memorials and artefacts

These were a significant part of the learning process for children and adults, reminding people of God's presence among them as their covenant God. Some examples would include:
- Places marked with stone cairns, for example, at the crossing-place of the Jordan described in Joshua 4:4–9.
- Altars marking special events, for example, the altar to unity built by tribes returning to live west of the Jordan, in Joshua 22:6–27.
- External memorials such as Jacob's Well, Abraham's burial cave and the ruins of Jericho.
- Artefacts within the home: for example, part of the law was kept in a small case called a *mezuzah* that was hung on each doorpost in a Jewish home. As one entered the room, one would touch the *mezuzah* as a symbol of bringing blessing to that home.

Celebrations

Consider the following examples of special occasions where the presence of children is recorded or commanded.
- **Sacrificial worship (Deuteronomy 12:1–32):** 'The Lord will choose a place somewhere in Israel where you must go to worship him. All

your sacrifices and offerings must be taken there, including sacrifices to please the Lord... You and your family and servants will eat your gifts and sacrifices and celebrate there at the place of worship, because the Lord your God has made you successful in everything you have done' (vv. 5–7).
- **Renewal of the covenant (Joshua 8:30–35):** At the renewal of the covenant at Mount Ebal, 'Joshua read all the words of the law—the blessings and the curses—just as it is written in the Book of the Law... to the whole assembly of Israel, including the women and children, and the aliens who lived among them' (vv. 34–35, NIV).
- **Seeking God's help in crisis (2 Chronicles 20:1–19):** In the face of the approaching army of Edom, Jehoshaphat addressed the assembly of Judah and Jerusalem, publicly seeking God's help. Included in the assembly were 'every man, woman and child of Judah' (v. 13).

The joyful celebrations, thanksgiving, gladness and feasting all created an atmosphere of integration of children in the covenant community. Children were met at the point of their basic needs and hence a learning experience took place that transferred the faith far beyond words.

Education in the covenant community

The Old Testament description of the covenant community assumed that children would grow up as participating and learning members of the community. What style of learning took place? The covenant community was striking for its lack of separate institutions for the education of children.
- The law established no schools.
- No individuals were set aside as teachers of the young.
- There were no theories of education.
- There was no specialist training designed to prepare children for life in the world, for they lived not in the world but in a theocracy.
- Children were under the direct rule of God who was not only the one they worshipped but also their judge, ruler and king (Isaiah 33:22).

Parents' concern was not so much for the welfare of the individual child as for the covenant relationship of the whole nation with God. It was this principle that governed the way children were educated.

Passing on the faith

Parents wanted to bring up children to receive the teaching they themselves had been given and in due course pass it on to the next generation:

These are things we learnt from our ancestors, and we will tell them to the next generation. We won't keep secret the glorious deeds and the mighty miracles of the Lord. God gave his Law to Jacob's descendants, the people of Israel. And he told our ancestors to teach their children, so that each new generation would know his Law and tell it to the next.
PSALM 78:3–6

That teaching would be the knowledge of God, his covenant and laws. As we have seen, the process began with circumcision as an initiation into the covenant. Even aliens who lived among the Israelites were circumcised (Genesis 17:23–27). But not all circumcised people were spiritually alive. Ishmael was circumcised although he was denied the blessings of the covenant given to Isaac (Genesis 17:20–23).

Who were the educators?

The responsibility for the education of children in the covenant community rested with the parents. In the early days of the child's life, it seems that the mother was more important as the chief educator, and the care of the infant was left to her. 'You know what's best' was Elkanah's comment when Hannah consulted him about Samuel (1 Samuel 1:23). As a child grew, so the father took on the training and nurturing role: 'Some day your children will ask... Then you will answer' (Deuteronomy 6:20–21).

REFLECTION
In what ways do you think the church should help parents in their task of educating their children?

So we can note that in the Old Testament the responsibility for the education of children lay with the parents and not with the worshipping community, although the festivals and cycle of the year helped them in their task.

As the parents had the main responsibility for passing on the story of the faith of the covenant community, it meant that they also had the important task of maintaining the relationship with God. To fulfil such a task, parents needed training. Parts of Deuteronomy and Proverbs are regarded as providing important guidelines for bringing up children. Below is an exercise to discover some guidelines in parenting as set out in Deuteronomy.

First of all, read Deuteronomy 4:1–10. List the qualifications demanded of parents in the covenant community. Then read Deuteronomy 6:1–9 and list directions for education, nurture and faith transfer. Check your answers with the suggestions below.

Parents must...
- hear, follow and be true to God's word
- hold fast to the Lord
- be near to God in prayer
- live righteously
- remember and teach their experience of God
- teach reverence for God

Teaching must be...
- long-lasting
- specific
- real
- applied
- interactive
- consistent

These directives were expected of ordinary parents committed to the covenant God. Central to the Jewish concept of ministry to children was the process of faith transfer. The analogy is a relay race with parents and children moving in the same direction, with the same purpose of carrying the faith and values of Israel into the future. Parents understood their responsibility for handing over the baton of faith successfully to their children, who in turn understood their responsibility of passing it to their children. The result of passing on these faith teachings was clearly seen: 'If you obey them, you will live, and you will go in and take the land that the Lord is giving you' (Deuteronomy 4:1).

REFLECTION
- How significant are the above principles and processes in parenting today?
- What can you learn from the above in helping your church to develop strategies in parenting?

Summary

The aim of this chapter was to examine some Old Testament perspectives on children, to help us in putting together a picture of childhood in the covenant community. We can conclude that:
- Like adults, children are born reflecting the image of God and therefore can relate to God spiritually. They are full human beings, not humans in the making, and so they are caught up in human sinfulness.
- Children are God's gift to the covenant community as part of his creation and signs of his blessing. In belonging to that community, they have essential roles to fulfil in ensuring the future of the covenant people of God. It is the responsibility of that community to nurture and protect their children in thankfulness.
- Such protection will be seen in providing food, clothing, shelter and health. It will also include sharing the story of God's love and action

and modelling his way of living. In other words, that protection will be holistic in caring for the total well-being of each child.
- The key to this total well-being will be the sense of belonging through roots in a community, being taught its history and learning together about its caring, saving Creator who loves everyone unconditionally.

Further action

Think of the nurture you received as a child, then compare and contrast your upbringing with the features of the Old Testament covenant community. How would you describe the strengths and weaknesses in the nurture you experienced? What implications does this bring for your ministry among children today?

Further study

The book of Proverbs has been described as a kind of education manual showing how the wisdom of God could be passed on to the new generation, a book of discipline and education for Jewish homes. Read through Proverbs. Keep a running account of every feature that has nurture implications, especially the understanding of the child's condition and the effect on his development of the company he keeps.

After your study, make notes on:
- Features that might be included in your ministry with children
- Features that could change your practice

The following books are recommended to help you with your reflection:
Derek Kidner, *Proverbs: an Introduction and Commentary* (IVP, 1974).
Eric Lane, *Special Children?* (Grace Publications Trust, 1996).

Chapter 2

CHILDREN FROM JESUS' PERSPECTIVE

In the previous chapter we looked at some Old Testament perspectives on children with their subsequent implications for children's ministry today. The purpose of this material is to focus on the value and importance that Jesus placed on children and the subsequent challenges for us in our ministry with children today. We shall look at some specific examples of how Jesus related to children and especially the profile he gave them.

By the end of this chapter we will have gained an overview of the Gospel passages relating to Jesus and children and will have been challenged afresh to review the guidelines in our work and relationship with children in the light of Jesus' attitude and actions.

Read the following passages to get an overview of what Jesus thought of children, and reflect on the questions at the end of each passage.

The little children and Jesus

Some people brought their children to Jesus, so that he could place his hands on them and pray for them. His disciples told the people to stop bothering him. But Jesus said, 'Let the children come to me, and don't try to stop them! People who are like these children belong to God's kingdom.'
MATTHEW 19:13–14 (SEE ALSO MARK 10:13–16)

- What did the people who brought their children to Jesus want?
- What did the disciples want?
- What did Jesus want?

Who is the greatest?

About this time the disciples came to Jesus and asked him who would be the greatest in the kingdom of heaven. Jesus called a child over and made the child stand near him. Then he said: 'I promise you this. If you don't change and become like a child, you will never get into the kingdom of heaven. But if you are as humble as this child, you are the greatest in the kingdom of heaven. And when you welcome one of these children because of me, you welcome me.'

MATTHEW 18:1–5 (SEE ALSO MARK 9:33–37)

- What can adult disciples learn from children?

A child like us

Jesus of Nazareth was born at a particular time in history and lived as a child in a particular context. He was born in a stable in Bethlehem; his parents were forced to become refugees in Egypt. He was brought up in Nazareth with his extended family. Although we have a record of his life, his ministry, his death and resurrection, we have no physical picture of him. Nevertheless, we do know that he grew up as any other child of his time.

Read the first two chapters of Luke and Matthew, which give a very human picture of his childhood and family relationships.

Developing as a child

The child Jesus grew. He became strong and wise, and God blessed him.
LUKE 2:40

Jesus became wise, and he grew strong. God was pleased with him and so were the people.
LUKE 2:52

Belonging to a family

Your relative Elizabeth is also going to have a son, even though she is old. No one thought she could ever have a baby, but in three months she will have a son.
LUKE 1:36

While Jesus was still speaking to the crowds, his mother and brothers came and stood outside because they wanted to talk with him.
MATTHEW 12:46

Jesus' mother stood beside his cross with her sister and Mary the wife of Clopas. Mary Magdalene was standing there too. When Jesus saw his mother and his favourite disciple with her, he said to his mother, 'This man is now your son.' Then he said to the disciple, 'She is now your mother.' From then on, that disciple took her into his own home.
JOHN 19:25–27

Participating in a worshipping community

Every year Jesus' parents went to Jerusalem for Passover. And when Jesus was twelve years old, they all went there as usual for the celebration. After Passover his parents left, but they did not know that Jesus had stayed on in the city. They thought he was travelling with some other people, and they went a whole day before they started looking for him. When they could not find him with their relatives and friends, they went back to Jerusalem and started looking for him there. Three days later they found Jesus sitting in the temple, listening to the teachers and asking them questions. Everyone who heard him was surprised at how much he knew and the answers he gave. When his parents found him, they were amazed. His mother said, 'Son, why have you done this to us? Your father and I have been very worried, and we have been searching for you!' Jesus answered, 'Why did you have to look for me? Didn't you know that I would be in my Father's house?' But they did not understand what he meant. Jesus went back to Nazareth with his parents and obeyed them. His mother kept on

thinking about all that had happened. Jesus became wise, and he grew strong. God was pleased with him and so were the people.
Luke 2:41–52

The fact that Christ, the Son of God, was truly human helps us in our humanity. He himself went through the stages of human development —birth and growth to maturity. He grew physically, in intellectual understanding, spiritually and socially. Jesus belonged to a family network, having younger brothers and sisters and an aunt Elizabeth and cousin John. Like any other Jewish boy he would have grown up within the community of God's covenant people, attended the synagogue and celebrated the Sabbath and Passover and so on.

How does it help in our work with children to know that Jesus was a child like us? Consider the following quotations:

> *For he is our childhood's pattern:*
> *day by day like us he grew;*
> *He was little, weak, and helpless,*
> *Tears and smiles like us he knew;*
> *And he feels for all our sadness,*
> *And he shares in all our gladness.*
> From 'Once in royal David's city', Cecil Frances Alexander

He had to be one of us, so that he could serve God as our merciful and faithful high priest and sacrifice himself for the forgiveness of our sins. And now that Jesus has suffered and was tempted, he can help anyone else who is tempted.
Hebrews 2:17–18

The world of Jesus

To understand the impact of Jesus' attitude to children, we need to be familiar with the cultural climate of his day. Jesus was born into a Jewish community during the height of the Roman Empire and was subject to the Jewish law:

But when the time was right, God sent his Son, and a woman gave birth to him. His Son obeyed the Law, so he could set us free from the Law, and we could become God's children.
GALATIANS 4:4–5

Jesus' world was also strongly influenced by Greek and Roman culture in which children had little worth in themselves as individuals except for the continuation of their family line and national identity. Contemporary writings tell us that sons were simply numbered, rather than named. The clearest indication of the low status of children is seen in the fact that they were easily disposable:

Offspring was not reared of the will of the father, but was taken and carried by him to a place called Lesche, where the elders of the tribes officially examined the infant. If it was well-built and sturdy, they ordered the father to rear it, and assigned it one of the nine thousand lots of land; but if it was ill-born and deformed, they sent it to the so-called Apothetae, a chasm-like place at the foot of Mount Taygetus, in the conviction that the life of that which nature had not well-equipped at the very beginning for health and strength, was of no advantage either to itself or to the state.
LYCURGUS 16:1FF. (QUOTED IN WEBER, *JESUS AND THE CHILDREN*)

Child-rearing was regarded as a preparation for future living, whether it were to defend the state (as with the Spartans), to develop the mind (as with the Athenians), or to become worthy citizens (as with the Romans).

Seen against this background, Jesus' reaction was radical. Jesus did not see children as raw material to be shaped in preparation for life. By his attitudes and actions, Jesus taught never to regard children on the basis of future worth, but to look at children as full human beings deserving of the care and concern of any adult as accepted members of the community. In his actions and words he reflected the Old Testament perspectives but at the same time brought a new focus—so new that even his disciples could not grasp it.

As we read through the Gospels, we will note four aspects of this focus—a new relationship, a new model, a new worth and a new challenge.

A new relationship

Unlike the many stories of children that we find in the Old Testament, when we come to the New Testament children appear infrequently as characters in the narratives of all four Gospels. Jesus' focus on children revolves round their worth both as members of their society and their relationship to God.

My Father, Lord of heaven and earth, I am grateful that you hid all this from wise and educated people and showed it to ordinary people. Yes, Father, that is what pleased you.
LUKE 10:21

In spite of the many needs around him, Jesus' ministry was built on relationship with individuals. The examples below show how Jesus built relationships with children.

Jesus involved children in his teaching

Consider the account of the feeding of the five thousand in John 6:1–15: 'There is a boy who has five small loaves of barley bread and two fish. But what good is that with all these people?' (v. 9). Jesus uses a boy to help him in performing one of his classic teaching miracles. It is worth noting that on no occasion do we find Jesus teaching children on their own. No doubt children were present with their parents at this event. Jesus was probably endorsing his own experience of learning within an all-age community, which was the pattern in the Old Testament. What does this say to us about the value of all-age activities?

Jesus cared for children's physical needs

Jesus was always willing to heal children on all occasions and responded whether they were girls or boys, whether the request for help was from a father or a mother, a Jew or a Gentile. Look up the following instances when Jesus healed children and note the circumstances in particular.

Jairus' daughter: Mark 5:21–24, 35–43
The Syro-Phoenician woman's daughter: Mark 7:25–30

The demoniac boy: Mark 9:14–27
The official's son: John 4:46–53

In each case, the request to Jesus comes from the parents, not from the children themselves. Why do you think that happened? What does this say to us about the significance of working with children in the context of family and carers?

Jesus encouraged children's worship

Consider the following passage:

But the chief priests and the teachers of the Law of Moses were angry when they saw his miracles and heard the children shouting praises to the Son of David. The men said to Jesus, 'Don't you hear what those children are saying?' 'Yes I do!' Jesus answered. 'Don't you know that the Scriptures say, "Children and infants will sing praises"?' Then Jesus left the city and went out to the village of Bethany, where he spent the night.
MATTHEW 21:15–17

As we see, when Jesus entered Jerusalem and the children themselves waved palms and cheered, and when this praise was taken up in the temple courtyards, it simply became too much for the religious authorities, who asked Jesus to stop the children shouting out. Jesus refused to do so since he wanted to endorse not only the worship and adoration from these children but also the fact that children anywhere could worship God for themselves. What does this say to us about our willingness to accept that children can relate to God spiritually in worship and lead adults in praise and adoration?

Jesus observed children at play

Look up the parable of the children playing in the marketplace in Matthew 11:16–19 and Luke 7:31–35. Note how the Gospel writers recall Jesus' use of an incident of children at play to illustrate how people had reacted to both Jesus himself and John the Baptist.

According to these accounts, Jesus saw in the children and their unsuccessful game a parable for those Jewish leaders who did not see that the coming of John the Baptist and Jesus heralded a decisive hour for their lives and for world history. The way Jesus treated children showed that he did not have a sentimental evaluation of them. In this particular parable, the children and their game significantly served as a mirror of the unbelief of the adults.

Jesus' approach to children can help us to rethink our priorities in life and to reverse much of our thinking. All of us have seen children at play. What strikes you most as you think of children playing together?

REFLECTION

Take these examples of the different ways in which Jesus developed new relationships with children. What guidelines do they give you in your ministry with children?

A new model

Through his words and actions Jesus encouraged his followers to recognize, value and learn from the qualities and characteristics present in children. Jesus welcomed and paid attention to children in what was an adult world. In Jesus' overall dealings with children, the Gospel accounts show a totally different model in his attitude towards children from that of his disciples. Jesus took time from a busy schedule to welcome children to come to him. Look again at Mark 10:13–16. It may be that the incident was linked to the custom of children asking for the blessing of famous rabbis, whatever the situation.

The disciples turned the children away. Some writers have surmised that it was to protect Jesus, as he may well have been tired. Whatever the case, the disciples were surprised to find that they had made the wrong decision when they tried to stop people bringing small children to Jesus for a blessing. The disciples had to learn quite a new concept: 'When you welcome even a child because of me, you welcome me. And when you welcome me, you welcome the one who sent me' (Mark 9:37).

In this verse, Jesus is asking that a child should be received as his representative. In Matthew's account we read that Jesus continued with a damning condemnation of any person who might cause a child to sin:

> It will be terrible for people who cause even one of my little followers to sin. Those people would be better off thrown into the deepest part of the sea with a heavy stone tied around their necks! The world is in for trouble because of the way it causes people to sin. There will always be something to cause people to sin, but anyone who does this will be in for trouble.
> MATTHEW 18:6–7

In effect, such people, in damaging the child as Jesus' representative, are showing their rejection of Jesus. Perhaps this is why Jesus cared for children—because they were a vulnerable and marginalized group, like the 'fatherless 'of the Old Testament. But also he cared for them because they belonged to God's kingdom and had something to teach adults as a model of discipleship. This was a huge paradigm shift in challenging the contemporary status of children. Such an attitude supports the thinking in the Church of England report *Children in the Way*: 'Jesus extended the traditional view of the young as those who are to be moulded and taught and offered them as those from whom we can also learn' (p. 3).

A new worth

The worth of children is enhanced by the way Jesus uses their lack of status and their powerlessness in society as the very credentials for entry to the kingdom of heaven:

> I promise you this. If you don't change and become like a child, you will never get into the kingdom of heaven. But if you are as humble as this child, you are the greatest in the kingdom of heaven.
> MATTHEW 18:3–4

The status of children as equal with adults is the significant affirmation of the biblical tradition as far as Jesus saw it. Even though there is still much potential growth for our children, childhood is real life and not just preparation for what is to come. The child will change, develop and grow but ought never to be treated on the basis of future worth. Jesus saw children as modest and unspoiled, compared with adults who could not receive him because of their pride (Matthew 18:2–5; 19:13–15). Adults had a tendency to disparage the child and block out God's love. But for Jesus, the children's size, immaturity and need of help meant that they were more open to receive and understand the fatherly love of God. Perhaps this is a frightening image for us to accept. God chooses to give the kingdom to the young because they are ready to receive it as they receive Jesus.

By his words, attitudes and actions, Jesus showed that he believed that children could belong to God's loving kingdom—and even that they had something to teach us as adults.

A new challenge

Jesus is saying that to be part of the kingdom of God, to follow him, it is necessary to become like a child. The child does not need to make any conscious effort to take a lowly place. He has no power and no status in terms of this world's values. Jesus was not advocating a false sense of humility but rather a proper dependence on the one in charge.

Look up Philippians 2:6–11. Jesus 'gave up everything and became a slave' (v. 7). In Aramaic the words 'slave' and 'child' are synonymous. Jesus, as God's own Son, became willing to take the place of a slave like a child, a place of no importance in the world's eyes, to fulfil God's purposes. Here we see Jesus' radical nature in his ministry towards the children of his day. For Jesus, a child as a person of worth and significance was a reminder of our need of God and our dependence on him.

Summary

The following poem was written by delegates at the *New Directions in Children's Ministry* Consultation at London Bible College in 1995. How does the poem summarize Jesus' approach to children?

If

If you are excluded from the family meal,
If you speak and no one listens but you cry and everyone 'tuts',
If you are sad but no one asks you what's the matter,
If you don't vote because your opinions are not valued,
If you can't read and you're expected to,
Or, if you can, you're not given a book,
If you have a faith and no one believes you,
If you come bearing gifts and no one accepts them,
If you are not getting value for money,
If you try your best for a right answer and only get a laugh,
If you bring your worship and everyone thinks it is entertainment

Then you are a child.

If you think the aisle is for cartwheels
If you can laugh at the preacher but not at his jokes,
If you say God is wicked and know it's OK,
If you don't care a toss about getting wet,
If just by your presence you bring others joy,
If you're prepared to take risks and questions,
If you are the role model for the Kingdom

Then you are a child.

Forward action

Reflect on the following quotation from *Children in the Way*:

If children are to continue in the way of faith, they must be aided and supported by adult fellow Christians who are also on that journey, and must be acknowledged as those who sometimes lead the way.

How can your church model a way of life to show that it supports children in their spiritual journey as equal travellers, allowing children sometimes to lead the way?

Chapter 3

CHILDREN IN THE EARLY CHRISTIAN COMMUNITY

In the light of the special focus children have in the ministry of Jesus in the Gospels, it is difficult to understand why so little is recorded about the place of children and their nurture in the early Christian community. The aim of this chapter is to attempt to build a picture of what was happening from a child's perspective in the early Church.

At the end of this chapter we will have gained an overview of a picture of a new Christian community struggling to find identity within a hostile society. Within that community we will have some insight into how its children were loved and nurtured in the Christian faith as part of its community life.

The early Church community was a new and growing community within the context of a hostile society. As it developed, the young Church challenged the culture of the day by living as a society that focused on a radical mutual concern for each other rather than on power and hierarchy. Women, children and servants were to be regarded no longer as nobodies but as important members of the kingdom of God. But the members of this young growing Church needed help to tackle some of their concerns. How should they relate to the wider society around? What about their Jewish neighbours? What about their Roman masters? How could they resist cultural pressures now that they were Christians? What about tensions of leadership in their new churches? Who should have authority? How should divisive matters of controversy and rivalry be addressed? How should families be helped in this new situation?

With such critical concerns, it was no wonder that the writings of the early Christian Church were problem-centred, with little attempt to produce a systematic doctrinal expression of faith and practice.

Furthermore, with so many other growing tensions for this new group of Christians, it is likely that matters concerning the place of children would not have been a priority. Perhaps this is why there is little mention about ministry with and to children. As we look for evidence of ministry to children, we are not going to find answers to such questions as baptism of infants, strategies for learning and nurture within the church community. But we can try to assess, through incidents and passing comments from the New Testament and early Christian writings, how the children in the New Testament Church were involved as part of the community.

REFLECTION

What does this say to us about the priorities of listening and building relationships with the child, the family, the community, organizations and agencies?

Children in the family context

It would seem that children were so much part of the Christian community, sharing its commitment to the Lord and involvement in its life, that Paul and others could address them directly in general letters to the churches, especially with regard to Christian relationships in the home.

Consider the following passages:

Christian relationships between children and parents: Ephesians 6:1–4
Christian households: Colossians 3:20–23

What picture do these passages give of children and their relationship to parents?

In these references we see a practical expression of Jesus' vision for the family, with children involved in the communal life of the Church, learning in the household and regarded as members of the Church with a role to fulfil and a special need of encouragement and support. Paul's instructions for good relationships were straightforward.

A two-way relationship

For Christian children, it would appear that Paul sees obedience to parents as a major responsibility. In fulfilling their obedience to parents, children were fulfilling their responsibility to their Lord. Paul is putting relationships between children and parents on a different basis. No longer is the relationship simply because of the biological link but because they are linked to each other 'in the Lord'.

Children, you belong to the Lord, and you do the right thing when you obey your parents.
EPHESIANS 6:1

Children must always obey their parents. This pleases the Lord.
COLOSSIANS 3:20

As far as parents were concerned, they were urged to develop a positive relationship with their children and to regard them not just as passive members, but as fellow members of the body of Christ equal with adults before God (but needing special care and nurture to help them grow towards maturity).

Parents, don't be hard on your children. Raise them properly. Teach them and instruct them about the Lord.
EPHESIANS 6:4

Parents, don't be hard on your children. If you are, they might give up.
COLOSSIANS 3:21

Church officials must be in control of their own families, and they must see that their children are obedient and always respectful. If they don't know how to control their own families, how can they look after God's people?
1 TIMOTHY 3:4–5

Here Paul urges Timothy to see good parenting as a qualification for being a leader in a church. It is unlikely that Paul was talking about good parenting as a matter of learning skills. He was more likely referring to the fact that if a Christian parent in leadership could not establish a Christian atmosphere in his own household, then what hope would that leader have in producing the right Christian atmosphere in the family of the church?

REFLECTION

- What does this picture of the church community tell us about the encouragement of parental responsibilities towards children and child-rearing in the community around them?
- The first letter to Timothy describes the faith community as God's household where there is a caring community of role models in managing their families. What does this say about strategies for helping parents today?
- What if they reject...? Children nurtured in a Christian context may well reject all they have had in terms of their background. How do you help parents in this situation?

Some early Christian writers

In searching for a picture of attitudes to children in the early Church, evidence from contemporary Christian writers gives an additional perspective. Below are some extracts to illustrate attitudes.

Let our children partake of the training that is in Christ. Let them learn how humility avails with God, what pure love can do with Him, how the fear of God is good and great and saves those who live therein in holiness and in pure mind.
CLEMENT, EPISTLE TO THE CORINTHIANS 21:7–8 (CIRCA AD110)

Let us teach, first of all, ourselves to walk in the commandments of the Lord. Next, teach your wives to walk in the faith given to them, and in love and in

purity to love their own husband in all truth, and to love all others equally in all chastity; and to train up their children in the knowledge and fear of God.
POLYCARP, EPISTLE TO THE PHILIPPIANS 4:2 (CIRCA AD150)

We must train the children to utter grave and reverent words. We must drive many strangers away, so that no corrupt men may also find their way in to mingle with these citizens. Words that are insolent and slanderous, foolish, shameful, common, and worldly, all these we must expel... Let their words be giving thanks, solemn hymns; let their discourse ever be about God, about heavenly philosophy.
CHRYSOSTOM, ON BRINGING UP CHILDREN, P. 99 (AD388)

Teach him to be fair and courteous. If thou dost see a servant ill-used by him, do not overlook it, but punish him who is free; for if he knows that he may not ill use even a slave, he will abstain all the more from insulting or slandering one who is free and of his class. Stop his mouth from speaking evil. If thou dost see him traducing another, curb him and direct his tongue towards his own faults.
CHRYSOSTOM, QUOTED BY LAWRENCE RICHARDS, CHILDREN'S MINISTRY, ZONDERVAN 1983, P. 100

REFLECTION

The above extracts are typical of much that was written about bringing up children. As you reflect on these passages, how would you assess the view of children described and the way they should be nurtured and disciplined? How does this compare with the view implied in the Old and New Testament writings?

Children in the Christian community

They spent their time learning from the apostles, and they were like family to each other. They also broke bread and prayed together. Everyone was amazed by the many miracles and wonders that the apostles performed. All the Lord's followers often met together, and they shared everything they had. They would sell their property and possessions and give the money to whoever needed it. Day after day they met together in the temple. They broke bread together in different homes and shared their food happily and freely, while praising God. Everyone liked them, and each day the Lord added to their group others who being saved.

Acts 2:42–47

Features of the Christian community

Focus on homes

One of the strongest arguments indicating children's participation in the life of the early church is the fact that the church community met within the home (see Romans 16:5).

The first Christians had no separate church building in which to meet. When they came together it was in the homes of church members and, of necessity, the children of those hosts and other families would be there when the church gathered together for worship and teaching. It would seem that their presence did not necessarily affect the form of worship but nevertheless children would have been present because they belonged there.

Focus on sharing

Look up the following texts:

Romans 12:6–8
1 Corinthians 12:7–11
Ephesians 4:11–13
Romans 15:14
Hebrews 10:23–26
1 Corinthians 14:26, 29–31
Romans 13:9–16

What do the passages tell us about the characteristics of this new Christian community?

Where did children fit in?

Such an all-inclusive community, devoted to Christ with an attitude of caring support for one another, must have been extended to children of the families of believers. Yet while the early Church designed nurture programmes for adult converts, there is nothing recorded that is similar for children. There were no Sunday schools, for Christian nurture took place within the home and the worshipping community. As far as ordinary education was concerned, the church community provided no Christian schooling for its children. Children from Christian families were normally educated in Greek and Roman schools through a secular curriculum. The implication of living within a secular society helped them to appreciate the difference between a pagan society and Christian community.

REFLECTION

What does this say about the role of Christian schools for us in today's postmodern society? How do we help our children in our church communities to cope with differing attitudes in their school communities?

Carrying the faith forward

However little we can glean about children in the early Church, we do know that the Church grew, as successive generations owned their commitment to Christ. Frequently, where children are mentioned in the New Testament it is in connection with being brought up in the faith.

As an example, consider the ways in which Paul helped the young Timothy to grow as a Christian. Paul tried to encourage Timothy to be aware that as a Christian he would meet opposition (2 Timothy 3:12) and to hold on to what he had been taught and knew to be true (2 Timothy

3:14). He reminded him of the influence of his mother and grandmother (2 Timothy 1:5) and to remember his early upbringing: 'Since childhood, you have known the Holy Scriptures' (2 Timothy 3:15).

REFLECTION

What does this say to you about the importance of the process of ongoing spiritual nurture for children both in the church and family life?

A summary

From the New Testament writings we can see in the early Church a new Christian community facing all the joys and problems of growth within a secular environment. Children were inevitably part of that community and were treated with the same all-inclusive love, care and nurture offered to adult members.

In terms of the present climate and culture in which we live, our circumstances can reflect something of life in the early Christian community. Our responsibilities to nurture and care for our children remain the same: even though the way we fulfil those responsibilities may change, the challenge to make children a priority in our church communities has lost none of its urgency.

Forward action

How can we best encourage children's ministry in our churches? How can we best keep our churches informed about the work we are doing with our children? How can we keep children on the church agenda?

SECTION TWO

How children grow

In this section we are going to focus on a number of significant studies in child development to help us understand how and why children behave and develop in faith as they do. Even if you have no formal knowledge of these subjects, you will probably have had the experience of interacting with children, and you will identify with the characteristics of different ages and stages of development. The aim of this section is that we will engage with the material and develop our own understanding of how children grow.

Chapter 4

WHATEVER HAPPENED TO CHILDHOOD?

Think of the word 'child'. Write down the first three words or images that come to your mind. Where do your images come from? Your own childhood... children you know... children around your neighbourhood... children you have seen in pictures...? Are they mostly negative or positive images, or are they neutral?

To what extent would you say you were influenced in your choice of images by the way you were brought up... by your memories of your own childhood... by the views of your parents... by the views of your relatives... your friends... your neighbours... your teachers and others in your community?

You may have been influenced by what you have seen or read. In other words, you have been influenced by your own experiences. You have also been influenced by the culture in which you have grown up, and this includes your ethnic background, social class and gender.

Now do the same for the word 'childhood'. Do you think in terms of this being a period of time? If so, when does it start and finish? Compare how you feel with someone from a different cultural background. What are their images of children and childhood? In what ways are their images the same as or different from yours?

Childhood—a historical perspective

Social historians have argued that 'childhood' has been created by society and is not a stage given in nature. Philippe Aries, in his research in *Centuries of Childhood* (Penguin, 1962), looked at the study of childhood from a historical perspective and put forward the thesis that 'childhood' as a separate stage of life was a discovery of the post-Renaissance society (p. 33). His conclusions have been challenged by subsequent writers, especially Shahar in his *Childhood in the Middle Ages*. In his writings Shahar examines attitudes towards children, images of childhood and concepts of the stages of childhood in medieval culture from the nobility to the peasantry. He claims that medieval scholars saw the child as different from the adult in ways other than size alone, and argues that Aries ignored the wider cultural context in which children were raised in the past. Whatever viewpoint is accepted, such thinking reminds us that previous ages may have had quite different perspectives about childhood from our own.

Childhood—a cultural perspective

Thinking about childhood as a time for play is a Western perspective. In many cultures, particularly in agricultural communities, childhood hardly exists. Children are expected to take part in the family's work as soon as they are able. Often bringing up younger siblings, they quickly learn adult responsibilities. In Western cultures, where parents usually work outside the home, children are largely cut off from the world of work, and education is about formal learning in a school setting. Play and learning in agrarian communities, where work is bound up with survival, tends to be about preparation for taking on adult roles.

Childhood—no uniform perspective

Perspectives about the significance of play and education differ even within the UK. Think of different areas within the UK (rural, suburban, urban, inner city). What different views might be found regarding play and education? Consider the following factors:
- social
- political
- economic
- spiritual

In Western society, the 19th century saw radical changes in the lives of children that clearly made childhood into a separate experience from the rest of life. From being an agrarian society in which parents were helped economically by the child, the West has become an industrial society where parents support the child but do not expect any support in return. Although childhood labour is still a problem in a large part of the world, it has disappeared over the past 150 years in the Western world. Shaftesbury's reforms played a major part in this change.

Traditionally, childhood in the West has become a period when children are considered too young to work. It is seen more as a time of preparation for adulthood. Childhood is a time to learn, to play and to be valued for the love that children themselves can give to adults. In recent years, with the United Nations Convention on the Rights of the Child and national legislation to implement it, there has been an increasing focus on the need to promote and safeguard the period of childhood. Such change has come about as a result of a number of factors, for example:

- The move to an industrialized society
- A change in relationship between parents and children, moving work out of the home
- The need for young people to be trained in new work skills, requiring training for entry into a competitive job market
- The rise of formal compulsory schooling outside the home

The effects of these changes mean that no longer are parents and the extended family the only educators for the child. The child acquires new skills, new values, and often a new social status. Medical advances have reduced mortality and birth rates, and no longer is a large family seen as necessary in an industrial society. In fact, a large family can lead to increased costs, as children are no longer able to give an economic return to the parents.

Childhood has become increasingly seen as a distinct and valuable period of life. This glimpse of a happier image of childhood highlights the tragedy that millions of children still live in difficult circumstances, deprived of a normal, healthy childhood. Children in much of the world are no longer provided with a living environment conducive to their happiness, growth and the special protection they need to promote and safeguard the period of childhood.

Chapter 5

CHILD DEVELOPMENT

In this chapter we shall explore what we mean by child development and examine the child's social world in terms of home and families, peer group and schools, community and environment. We will consider how a child's thinking develops and, in the light of the above, think about our own childhood and identify and explore some of the changes which have taken place since we were young and the effect these changes have on our work with children.

By the end of this chapter we will have considered various studies and theories as to how children develop from a social and cognitive perspective and seen how to apply such thinking to work with children in the church.

REFLECTION

Write down a definition of the word 'development'. Underline the key words as you see them. When you have read this chapter, reconsider your definition. Do you feel you correctly identified the key words? Are there words you would now add to or subtract from your definition?

What do we mean by 'development'? Is the birthday a mark of developmental progress? Suppose it is my birthday tomorrow. Tonight I go to bed as a nine-year-old. Tomorrow I will wake up as a ten-year-old and will be allowed to stay up another hour. The child who is still nine might see this as unfair.

Is the school starting date a mark of developmental progress? What about the five-year-old who can start school and the child a few weeks younger who can't? Such age divisions take no account of difference between individuals. It just seems easier for adults to plan things that way.

Not ages but stages

Educators do not talk about ages but stages of development. All of us use different life-skills at different developmental stages, which tend to follow a sequence. For example, you can't use a word processor if you do not know the alphabet. You can't ride a bicycle before you have learnt to walk. As well as life-skills, we have spiritual and emotional skills. For example, if we cannot trust the people who take care of us, we will find it hard to trust God.

To be effective leaders, we need to understand children's development in terms of these stages and anticipate the often-turbulent transition from one stage to another.

A definition of development

Peter Smith and Helen Cowie, in their excellent summary of current psychological research *Understanding Children's Development* (Second edition, Blackwell, 1991), define development as the process by which an organism (human or animal) grows and changes throughout its lifespan. In humans, the most dramatic developmental changes occur in infancy and childhood as the newborn baby develops into a young adult, capable of becoming a parent himself or herself (p. 5). As leaders, parents, brothers, sisters, teachers and friends, those living and working with children, we all observe and comment on the ways in which children grow, develop and change. Those studying child development are interested in the many factors involved in these changes: pre-natal experiences, patterns of early care, the experience of schooling, the influence of the peer group and so on. All of these factors link in countless combinations to make us into the adults we eventually become.

Developmental psychologists often divide up the study of the process of development into two main areas:
- The study of the child's social world: this includes the influence of parents, carers, brothers and sisters, families, friends and school; the value of play; the development of children's emotions and their social understanding.
- The study of the child's mind or cognitive development: this includes how thinking, perception and language develop, and looks at issues to do with how a child learns, the development of intelligence, the memory, reasoning and so on.

A process of growth

An understanding of the processes and issues involved in child development is foundational to working effectively with children in any context. But, as those involved in work with children within a Christian setting, it is paramount that we are aware of the social world in which today's children find themselves. We also need to understand how children's thinking develops, so that what we offer children is real and relevant. We shall be exploring aspects of the child's social world and the child's mind to help us understand how children grow.

But first let's look again at the process of growth as far as Jesus was concerned. Jesus, by becoming human, experienced birth, infancy, childhood and adolescence, and, as we saw in Section One, went through all the normal developmental processes.

Look up Luke 2:42 and 52. In the light of these passages, think again about Jesus' childhood and his relationship with his parents. Recognizing that Jesus had a normal childhood development, what do you imagine it might have been like for him growing up with his parents, Joseph and Mary?

Chapter 6

THE CHILD'S SOCIAL WORLD

A gradual revolution has taken place in the last decade. In developmental psychology, we think of a child as a social being—playing and talking with others, learning through interactions with parents and teachers. Alongside this, through that social interaction in which the child comes to understand the world, we see him or her making sense of experience and becoming a competent social individual, able to relate to the particular culture in which he or she lives.

Let us consider what factors shape our view of the world. In the centre of a sheet of paper, draw a figure to represent yourself as a child. Now draw some concentric rings around yourself. Think of all the influences upon you as a child—people and things—and place them somewhere on the rings, either nearer to or further from you, depending on their influence. You may like to include grandparents, parents, teachers, toys, environmental features (for example, trees and parks), friends, pets and places. To assess the impact of these influences, share them with another leader in your team.

Now think of a child you know well, and try to do the same for him or her. (This exercise may tell you something about how well you think you know the child as compared with how well you actually know him or her!) Children today are probably living in a very different world from the one we might have lived in when we were young. If we are to understand our children it is important we do not look at them in isolation from their social world, but see them as part of a number of larger systems—for example:
- Home
- School and peer group
- Community
- Environment

Look back at your own rings of influence. How many of the influences you identified as having had an impact on you can you see fitting into these systems?

The child's social world—the home

The whole cultural scene as far as 'home' is concerned is changing. Let's look at some examples of the way that is happening.

First of all, families, the backbone of the nation, are breaking up. At one time the home provided a sanctuary where the world did not intrude. The word 'family' is now difficult to define. For many children, 'family' means moving to another place in a process of restructuring. With this restructuring there is a sense of dislocation. Where is my home? Where do I belong? Who cares for me? On whom can I depend? Who will give me the nurture and training I need for my development? Where is that trusting relationship so important for my sense of security?

The need for an 'attachment relationship'

A newborn baby is helpless, vulnerable and dependent on adult care-givers for food, warmth and protection. The baby will respond to the sound and movement of an adult carer, whoever that may be. Nine months later, through interaction with the mother, the response towards a stranger will have changed. The baby's responses to the mother will now be very different from his responses to a stranger. An 'attachment relationship' has been put in place.

John Bowlby, in his 'maternal deprivation' hypothesis, *Child Care and the Growth of Love* (Harmondsworth, 1953, 1969), stated:

What is... essential for mental health is that the infant and young child should experience a warm, intimate and continuous relationship with his mother (or permanent mother-substitute—one person who steadily 'mothers' him) in which both find satisfaction and enjoyment.

His proposal, formulated in the post-war years when mothers were being encouraged to return to homemaking, was based on observations of young children separated from their parents while in short-term care. More recent evidence, however, has challenged his hypothesis. The notion of the importance of attachment to just one care-giver (the mother) has been disputed. Research has indicated that what is important for the child at this early stage of development is to have one or two consistent care-givers with whom he or she can build up a bond of security and trust. Mother, father or carer can fulfil this role.

Care outside the family

What would you think is the criterion for the primary care-giver? To be available and responsive to the child? To provide a secure, consistent environment?

Subsequent research has also re-evaluated the effects of long-term institutional care, suggesting that it is the nature of the care rather than the separation from the mother that contributes to the positive or negative effects on the child.

Despite the rejection of his 'maternal deprivation' hypothesis, Bowlby's work has highlighted a number of issues that remain significant in considering the early development of the infant. For example, there has been a reassessment of patterns of institutional care, as well as of hospital and day care, and an awareness of the child's emotional needs and of the long-term impact of bonding in early years.

Internal working models

Some research has suggested that children build up in their minds internal representations of 'early attachment' relationships, called internal working models. Internal working models are cognitive structures based on the day-to-day interactions with the mother (or other caregiver) and on the expectations and emotional experiences associated with these interactions. As the child grows older, this working model changes to account for new relationships and experiences. Where a child experiences a secure attachment and relationship, her or his internal working model of care-givers will be that they model behaviours which are available and responsive.

Where the experience has been of an insecure attachment, with inconsistent and unresponsive behaviours, this has implications for the child's later social and emotional development. While this theory cannot be applied uncritically to attachment patterns in adult life, it can be seen to provide a useful framework for thinking about the long-term effects of early attachment experiences.

REFLECTION

Think back to your own childhood and to the different forms of care arrangements you might have experienced—for example, care by parents, grandparents, adoptive parents, child minders, older siblings, or neighbours. Which of these were positive experiences? Why? Which were negative? Why? Can you identify any effects these experiences might have had on you in later life?

Widening relationships

As the child grows older, so the circle of adult carers expands beyond the primary care-givers to include siblings, grandparents, aunts and uncles and eventually child minders, day-care staff, and teachers and church leaders. Each of these expansions pushes out the horizons of the child, fulfilling different roles for him or her.

Influence of siblings

The relationship with siblings—brothers and sisters—is particularly important to the developing child. Judy Dunn has carried out extensive research into sibling relationships, showing how important brothers and sisters are as social partners, and the rich and complex relationships they have with each other. Her research has revealed a depth of emotion and understanding between siblings, often a love/hate relationship.

Judy Dunn challenges the thinking that age, gender and birth order are crucial factors, and asserts:

Children act towards their siblings as friends, supporters, comforters, and as playmates skilled at entering the fantasy world of the other, not only as disparaging bullies and as unkind aggressors... It is because they understand

their siblings so well, and because they feel so strongly about them, that their relationship is so significant and so revealing.
MAKING SENSE, ED. BRUNER AND HASTE, ROUTLEDGE, 1987, P. 26

Think of the brothers and sisters in your group. To what extent do their relationships support Dunn's research?

Fathers and grandparents

Both fathers and grandparents can also play key roles in the child's early development. Traditionally, grandparents have often been involved in childcare, supporting the parents and child emotionally and practically.

In addition, the role of grandparents in passing on family history and values is important. These days, the image of grandparents as elderly and largely inactive has been replaced by the image of grandparents in their sixties, still active and often still working.

Increasing research in recent years into the role of fathers in bringing up children has indicated that the majority of fathers are present at the birth of their children and are involved in many aspects of post-natal care. The employment market has also impacted this aspect of childcare in that, in some families, the mother is the principal wage earner while the father has become the 'houseparent'.

REFLECTION

Ask the leader of your creche to keep a diary over a period of time to show how children react with different helpers. What does this say to us about continuity of helpers?

The impact of divorce

The high rate of divorce means that children's and young people's leaders cannot overlook the matter. By the age of 16, there is a chance that one in three young people will have experienced divorce. While there is little evidence regarding the number of Christian divorces, there is a suggestion that one child in eight in a Christian home will experience divorce during the period they are involved with Sunday activities. What should we be doing to help children whose parents are going through divorce? How can we help children trust God as Father when they have no father in their lives? How do our teaching and learning programmes deal with these question?

REFLECTION

Bearing in mind the above discussion, make a list of the possible effects (positive as well as negative) on children and young people of some of the following trends, which are characteristic of life in the UK in the 21st century:

- Fall in number of married couples and increase in cohabitation.
- Rise in divorce rate.
- Rise in number of lone-parent families (22 per cent with dependent children are lone-parent families).
- Increased access to leisure-time activities.
- Increase in fast food and reduction in families who regularly eat meals together.
- Increase in homes where children have their own televisions and access to a personal computer.
- Increase in children living in families where the income is below half of the contemporary average income (1.4 million in 1979; 4.2 million in 1992/3).
- 100,000 under-16s run away from home each year.
- 42 per cent of young people brought before magistrates courts have been excluded from school.
- One in six children between 11 and 15 use drugs. They are five times more likely to truant and be excluded from school and be in trouble with police.
- Only one in five of all young people feel part of their local community.

(Figures taken from the *NCH Action for Children Factfile 1998*; *Still Running*, The Children's Society, 1999; 'The independent effects from permanent exclusion from school on the offending careers of young people', *RDS Occasional Paper No 71*; *Effective Drug Work*, Drug Scope 2001; *The Industrial Society, the 2002 Vision Summary Report*, The Industrial Society, 1997.)

Summary

The impact on the child of early experiences within the home cannot be under-estimated. Note in particular:
- The nature of the 'attachment relationships' the child has built up with the parent or primary care-giver
- The nature of the 'internal working model' that has been developed
- The range of social and psychological support available to the parents and to other family members
- Whether the child is of an easy or difficult temperament

All of the above factors combine to create a helpful or unhelpful context within which the child's early development takes place.

The child's social world—peer group and school

School has a tremendous impact on the lives of children. Children attend school for 39 weeks of the year. They spend six and a half hours a day in school. They sleep between nine and ten hours.

Most children move away from home-centred relationships to build up relationships with their peers in different contexts, particularly at school. A peer is someone who is about the same age as a given child, or in the same class or year group at school. During this period, issues to do with friendship, acceptance, aggression, self-esteem, status and conformity become significant for them.

Stages in social relationships

Research suggests that there are a number of stages to social relationships among children across the age span.

Infants appear to be interested in other children, although this interest is mainly limited to looking at one another. It takes up to two to three years for children to begin to interact socially. Even at nursery school, interaction in the first years (3–4) is mainly confined to solitary or parallel play (playing alongside but not with other children).

However, co-operative or group activity increases as the child becomes older (5–6), and the size of the co-operating group increases in middle childhood, especially among boys.

By the age of 7–8, the sharing of common activities and interests and living near to friends is seen as important. By these years also, segregation by sex of children's groups is becoming much more marked and there are differences in the types of activities favoured by the two groups. Boys tend to prefer larger groups, competitive team games with complex rules and roles, emphasizing issues to do with co-operation, competition and leadership, while girls prefer smaller groups or pairs with more emphasis on intimacy and exclusivity.

By the age of 9 and 10, the sense of belonging and of shared values and rules is seen to be important. These patterns continue into early adolescence.

By the age of 12–14, the nature of peer group interaction changes again as heterosexual relationships become more important. As adolescence progresses, aspects such as loyalty, commitment and mutual sharing, leading to intimacy, are seen as increasingly important.

REFLECTION

Think of the range of children's activities available at a church you know well. Find out about the various groups and jot down the age span within each group and the types of activities provided. Look back at the summary above. Would you say the types of groups and the activities offered are age-appropriate? Why or why not?

> Does it appear that those organizing the groups have an understanding of how opportunities for social interaction need to differ from age group to age group, or are they following their own ideas about what children of a given age group might like or 'need'?

The brief summary above refers to social interaction among peers. It should be noted that this is not the same as friendship, in that a child might interact with a lot of children but might not necessarily have any friends. Friendship involves a psychological attachment and trust. While it is not possible to make a direct link between the experience of close, stable friendships in the development of social skills and a positive self-concept, research does seem to indicate that the two are related. It may be seen that as children grow older, so they also gradually develop a sense of their own identity. This is influenced by a range of factors—their appearance, their personality, their skills and abilities, as well as by their gender and their ethnic background. In a school context, a child's self-identity is affected by issues to do with being popular, being accepted, conformity to certain peer group norms and so on. Thus, the experience of positive, stable friendships helps to contribute to a child's overall sense of self-worth.

Effect of teaching styles

Think of the importance of adult models. *Children in the Way* quotes the statement, 'I don't remember much that I learnt, but I remember the one who taught me.' As well as the influence of their peer group, the attitudes and expectations of the child's teachers are crucial. What do you remember about your first teacher in school? There is no doubt that teaching styles can affect the performance of children. Where a teacher believes that a child can do well and work hard, the child will attempt to respond accordingly, but where a teacher sees a child as unable, inarticulate and unco-operative, the child will tend to behave in this way, thus fulfilling these expectations. To what extent can the same thing be true for you as a children's or young people's leader in church?

REFLECTION

Think about your own experiences at school, at church or with friends and teachers. What aspects of these experiences contributed to helping you build a positive self-image? What aspects had a negative impact? How have you overcome the negative aspects? To what extent are you still affected by your experiences?

Can you recall one teacher who had a significant impact on you as a child/teenager? Was this a positive or a negative impact? For what reasons do you think they had this impact on you?

Now, if appropriate, think about your experience of leaders in Sunday activities. What impact did they have on your life?

The social world of the child—community and environment

Look out of your window or around you. Make a list of the good and bad features of your immediate environment—things you can see. Are you in a place that 'feels' good to be in? Are there features that pull you down or lift you up? Consider the following questions:

- If a child lives in a human-made environment, with little opportunity to see and appreciate natural beauty, what happens to the innate sensitivity to awe and wonder?
- If there is a continual exposure to vandalism, graffiti and lack of respect for property, what does this do in terms of lowering self-respect and respect for the neighbourhood?
- If a child constantly receives messages that it is not a priority to care for his or her community, how does this affect his or her value of that community?
- If a child grows up surrounded by damaged trees and plants, or public facilities left unrepaired, how does that child learn to develop respect for his or her area and for himself or herself?
- If a child grows up with a sense of powerlessness, knowing that decisions regarding the community are taken elsewhere, what motivation is there for trying to improve the environment?

There are clear moral reasons why efforts to end environmental degradation must focus on children... Children are too often the victims of pollution—their young bodies must make them far more vulnerable than adults. They and those yet to be born will inherit the earth we leave them. Their futures are in our hands—only we can protect it for them.
UNICEF/UNEP, 1990

Consider the different types of communities where children grow up.
- A wealth of multi-cultural richness: shops, clothing, foods, worship
- A mobile family pattern: extended family living at a distance
- A breakdown of community: no contact with neighbours
- Lack of focus for community: new estates and 'dormitory towns'
- Increase in superstores and shopping malls: loss of corner shops
- Local police presence replaced by the cruising police car
- Fear of 'stranger danger': parents do not permit children to play in streets and drive them from place to place rather than allowing them out in the neighbourhood

If we want to understand children today and learn to relate to them effectively, we need constantly to be aware of the impact that these systems have on their lives, and we need to realize that they are living in a different world to that in which we grew up.

REFLECTION

Take two newspapers, one a broadsheet and one a tabloid, and cut out all the articles and pictures to do with children. What do they say to you about the influences on a child today, about the world in which children are growing up? How do the different newspapers present different views of children?

Make a point of watching Saturday morning children's television or after-school children's programmes. Find out which are the most popular television programmes with children today. Don't omit soaps and chat shows! Read some latest examples of the magazines and comics your group are reading at present. Encourage them to do a critique.

> **Hire a video.** Do some investigations in your local video shop about the sort of videos children are hiring.

Consider the following extract from the *Daily Mail* (20 June 2000). What does this tell you about the impact of violence?

The cartoon is bugged by a rising tide of violence: They have always been seen as a harmless entertainment, an innocent if boisterous way of keeping children amused. But according to American academics cartoons are guilty of a huge rise in brutality. Animated violence has increased by more than 50 per cent since the release of Snow White and the Seven Dwarfs in 1937.

A Bug's Life has been rated the second most gory cartoon ever released, second only to a Quest for Camelot. Of the 74 films surveyed there were 125 injuries, 62 of them fatal. Characters portrayed as bad were 23 times more likely to die than good characters.

Researchers watched 74 cartoon videos, cataloguing every bash and smash.

Further action

Find out how your local community engages with children and young people. To what extent do children and young people have a say in what happens in your area? Do they have safe places to play? Look for agencies that offer children and young people a role in regenerating their communities and give them your support. You could also consider contacting agencies to work with—for example, Local Authority youth workers, Local Council representatives, Board for Social Responsibility, Community Matters, Early Years Partnership schemes and so on.

Chapter 7

HOW CHILDREN THINK

Compare the experience of working both individually and with a small group on a new learning task to explore and understand a particular chapter in the Bible.

There should be space in the group for each person to share their ideas and insights regardless of background, with plenty of encouraging support and no sense of 'put down'. What are the advantages and disadvantages of these two different approaches to learning?

When we hold a newborn baby in our arms, we may wonder what he or she is thinking and when this little one will be able to interpret external stimuli. What active part does the baby play in the process and how is he or she affected by environmental influences?

Read Paul's words to the Corinthian church in 1 Corinthians 13:11. What does it mean to think like a child, to reason like a child? Paul's own self-understanding made him aware that his thinking and reasoning processes had developed from childhood to adulthood. Perhaps we might try to look back and identify how our own thinking has developed.

The study of children's mental and intellectual development has been profoundly influenced by the work of the Swiss psychologist, Jean Piaget (1896–1980). While many aspects of his theories are now challenged and have been modified, few would deny the invaluable contribution he made to our understanding of the way in which children think.

Piaget's research had a major impact on the field of education. He encouraged the development of a child-centred approach to education, arguing that children thought differently from adults and viewed the world from a different perspective. He also encouraged the idea of active learning—learning by discovery, where the focus should be on the learning process rather than the outcome. In this the child sets the pace and the teacher is the guide.

Stages of thinking

Piaget saw children as 'little scientists' in the world, making and testing various hypotheses to understand their environment. He suggested that children go through four stages in the development of their thinking and that they do so in the same invariable order. Within these stages, changes in the structure of the children's intelligence takes place. These structures Piaget called 'schema' or 'mental operations', and they can be applied to any idea or activity in the child's world. As the child's thinking develops, so the structures evolve from one stage to the next.

In the first stage, *sensori-motor* (ages 0–2), the infant begins physically to act on her environment. She begins to learn about her world through her actions and her senses. In the second and third stages, *pre-operational* (ages 2–7), and *concrete-operational* (ages 8–11), she learns to form internal representations of these actions. They become symbols in the mind, but they are still closely tied to the physical, to concrete objects. In the fourth stage, *formal-operational* (11+), the child learns to work with these representations as abstract or hypothetical problems, divorced from the original concrete situations. The key point is that only from age 11 or 12 does a young person develop the ability to conceptualize, that is, to do what we usually mean by 'thinking'. Therefore only at adolescence and as adults can we construct or understand theory, philosophy or theology.

There are some significant points that need to be noted from Piaget's thinking:
- A young child cannot look at the world or a particular action from someone else's point of view.
- The question 'why?' is understood only after the age of 11 or 12 at the earliest. Before then, it will be answered in terms of cause or motive or justification (rules and customs).
- The ability to see events in chronological relationship down through the years usually develops around ages 10 or 11. While young children can be taught to say abstract words, such verbal ability should not be confused with what a child thinks or understands.

Too much too soon

If any one person was responsible for making teachers in the UK conscious of Piaget's 'stages' in religious thinking, it must be Ronald Goldman. His research was very much influenced by Piaget. As he applied Piaget's work to the religious thinking of children and adolescents, Goldman's work was widely reported, and the evidence he presented of children's difficulties in understanding biblical concepts not only proved to be psychologically illuminating as to how children learn, but also had a practical bearing on the structure and content of Agreed Syllabuses and the teaching of religion and Religious Education generally. In his research, he reported substantial investigations of religious thinking by children aged 6 to 16 years. For example, he devised a questionnaire using pictures and Bible stories (Moses and the burning bush, the crossing of the Red Sea, and the temptations of Jesus). The questionnaire revealed gross misunderstandings of basic religious concepts. For example, in reply to the question, 'Why was Moses afraid to look at God?' (Exodus 3:5–6), young children made wild guesses: 'God had a funny face'; 'He hadn't spoken politely'; 'He was frightened by the rough voice.'

Goldman noted that at the concrete stage of mental development (generally from 7 to 10), children dealt with cause and effect but concentrated on the specific situation and missed its meaning: 'He thought God would chase him off holy ground because he had shoes on'; 'Moses hadn't been going to church, or anything like that.' Only at the age of 11 or 12, when abstract thinking is thought to be possible, did children show any theological insights. Two 13-year-olds said, 'The awesomeness and mightiness of God would make Moses feel like a worm in comparison'; 'Moses would have a feeling of awe.'

When describing God, 6-year-olds used physical terms; 11- to 12-year-olds used superhuman categories; and 14-year-olds said you could not describe God because he can't be seen (R. Goldman, *Religious Thinking from Childhood to Adolescence*, Routledge, 1964). From this research, Goldman concluded that such biblical teaching was suited only to secondary school children, or possibly to more competent children in the final year of primary school.

Goldman's research had an enormous impact in the 1960s. The positive contribution of his work was to make educators in the church more careful about the content they presented to children and more aware of how children think. It is easy to see why this was so, as his work was based on what was at the time unusually careful research in the field of Religious Education and development. His publications, *Religious Thinking from Childhood to Adolescence* in 1964 and its sequel, *Readiness for Religion: A Developmental Basis for Religious Education* in 1965, were readable, with illustrative anecdotes, which fitted Goldman's picture. However, the findings lent themselves readily to sweeping and provocative generalizations about implications (such as 'Don't teach the Bible to children'). The result was that nearly a generation of Religious Education teachers and nearly all existing Christian Education and Religious Education programmes felt under attack. If Goldman's research was true, then there would need to be drastic adjustments within the teaching of Religious Education.

Again and again, Goldman insisted that the Bible is not a child's book and that 'too much too soon' only invited boredom and confusion. This was the beginning of a fierce debate which was to divide practitioners in the field of Religious Education. In 1966 Ken Howkins published a critique of Goldman's research and conclusions in his pamphlet *Religious Thinking and Religious Education* (Tyndale Press, 1966). His major criticism was that he felt that Goldman's own particular theological position and views on biblical interpretation had affected the criteria he used for assessing the children's responses. It was, for instance, Goldman's view that an Old Testament story could be fully understood only at a purely abstract, symbolic level which rejected any literal or historical appreciation of the story. This viewpoint, Howkins believed, would have an important influence on the way Goldman assessed the children's thinking and, in many ways, interpretations that he regarded as immature would be perfectly acceptable from a conservative theological viewpoint (*Religious Thinking and Religious Education*, pp. 24f.).

Another aspect that Goldman's studies left unresolved was the issue of how important this very consciously cognitive analysis of religious development was in any overall understanding of children's growth. Most children's leaders will know that young children can have imaginative, concrete ideas of God that will not compare favourably on theological grounds with adult concepts. But accepting that as given, there seems to be a world of difference between children who fear or dislike the God they know concretely or literally and children who like and trust Jesus as their friend. As other studies show, attitudes as well as ideas are learned.

In the late 1970s, books appeared that reflected something of a corrective reaction to Goldman's work. Edward Robinson's *The Original Vision: A Study of the Religious Experience of Childhood* (Seabury Press, 1977) affirmed the capacity that children have for deeply spiritual experiences. Goldman's work had led educators to discount children's abilities and capacities for religious understanding. Robinson and his team at the Religious Experience Research Unit in Oxford established a necessary corrective. A further stream of literature followed, including work inspired by Maria Montessori—Sofia Cavelletti's *The Religious Potential of the Child* (LTP, 1992). The introduction was written by Jerome Berryman, who developed his own approach to Christian education through the Godly Play movement (see p. 137).

As well as failing to take account of the spiritual background of the child, Goldman has also been criticized as giving insufficient weight to the social context within which a child learns. One of his critics, Margaret Donaldson, wrote on this subject in her book *Children's Minds* (Fontana, 1987), raising a number of issues which have an important bearing on how we understand and work with children. For example, she stresses the need to consider the whole child when seeking to explore what a child understands or is able to do. Donaldson observes that assessing a child as a standardized task in a laboratory setting may not present the full picture of what the child understands and can do. More can be learned by watching how the child responds in a natural setting, one with which the child is comfortable and familiar.

She also states that it is important to consider a situation from the child's point of view. In an experimental setting, the child is actively trying to make sense of what the adult is asking him or her to do. The child may well be responding to what he or she thinks the adult must mean rather than what is actually said or asked.

Finally, while affirming the importance of formal education—the need for a child to learn to work with abstract modes of thought—

Donaldson suggests that we need to understand that, for children, thinking is 'embedded' in its context. It needs to make 'human sense' to the child and it needs to take account of what the child is bringing to the situation. In contrast, our education system places value on 'disembedded' or abstract thinking. Margaret Donaldson suggests that we need to help our children move from one form of thinking to the other without devaluing the richness of thinking that children bring to a situation from their 'human sense perspective'.

You may wish to consider reading *Children's Minds* by Margaret Donaldson and apply her thinking to your work with children.

REFLECTION

Be a fly-on-a-wall in a Sunday group and observe how child-centred the leader is. To what extent is there an attempt to have things make 'human sense' to the child and to relate things to the child's world?

Review your teaching session to assess whether the children's openness and interest is being nurtured or discouraged by the way in which they experience the session.

Consider whether the language used is too abstract. Use the following exercise to measure your response by writing explanations of the following theological words in suitable language for younger and older children.

	Under 8s	Over 8s
Mercy		
Faith		
Church		
Worship		
Sin		

Alongside Goldman, Piaget has been challenged in a number of areas. His methods of research have been criticized for their artificial, experimental settings and for being too dependent on the skills and approaches of the interviewer, which makes replication difficult.

Another major challenge to Piaget's theories has come from the Russian psychologist, Lev Vygotsky (1896–1934). Like Piaget, he sees the child as active in constructing knowledge for himself. However, he asserts that the child does this through interaction with another person—usually an adult—who will 'arrange' experience for the child, encouraging him to note key variables, to look for explanations and to make sense of the experience.

Vygotsky suggests that there is a 'zone of proximal development' (ZPD), which he identifies as the gap between the actual developmental level of the child and his potential level of development. Provided that the child has the help of a more knowledgeable adult, it is within this zone that learning can take place, building upon the child's actual skills and knowledge and enabling the child to move on to learn new things.

Thus, as the child's understanding grows, so the 'scaffolding' of questions and prompts is slowly removed. This approach stresses the role of social interaction—the intervention of the adult (or peer) who challenges the child to move on to new knowledge by means of the relationship—as key to the child's developing understanding. The importance of the relationship and the interaction that takes place with the adult is crucial.

Summary

- Piaget states that children think differently from adults.
- Donaldson suggests that the whole child matters and that children need things to make 'human sense' to them.
- Vygotsky emphasizes the importance of an adult coming alongside the child and 'scaffolding', or providing supports, in the learning process.

Chapter 8

SPIRITUALITY AND FAITH DEVELOPMENT

In this chapter we shall be exploring what we mean by faith and what we mean by spirituality. We shall then consider ways in which we can nurture spirituality in children. Aspects of how children grow in faith will be discussed, helped by a consideration of some theories of faith development. Finally, we shall reflect on the practical implications for ministry with children.

We'll begin the chapter with two questions. First of all, at what point would you say you made a personal commitment of faith in Christ? Secondly, when in your life do you think you were first aware of God?

In the past twenty years, the work of faith development educators has had considerable impact in helping us understand how we grow in faith. If we can grasp something of the processes suggested in faith development, we will be helped in nurturing spirituality and faith in our children.

Think of three children you know of different age groups. As an example we will consider a 10-year-old called Tom, a 6-year-old called Sarah and 4-month-old Bethany. If faith requires some cognitive understanding and response, how can children understand spiritual truth when they are too young to make a cognitive decision? What does it mean when 10-year-old Tom tells you that he knows God helped him in school last week? Or when 6-year-old Sarah says she loves Jesus? As for 4-month-old Bethany, she can hardly speak, let alone express herself rationally, so how can she experience God? Can we describe any of these children as Christian?

So what sort of faith might they have? In your mind take the opportunity to think about children you know in the same age groups. What do you think would be the signs of having faith? What signs of faith would you look for in each age group?

Spirituality and faith

When considering whether children can be aware of God at an early age, the following passages may be of help. What do they tell us about children's spirituality?
- The boy Samuel (1 Samuel 3)
- Naaman's wife's servant girl (2 Kings 5:1–3)
- King Joash, the boy king (2 Kings 12)

If children were not able to understand and respond to spiritual truths, why would God have given these commands to parents? Reconsider Jesus' attitude to children in the adult-oriented world in which he lived. Why did Jesus emphasize the ability of children to understand spiritual matters when he praised God for revealing such truths to little children? (Matthew 11:25, NIV). What did Jesus mean when he said that the scrip-tures say that children and infants will sing praises? (Matthew 21:16). Compare this with Psalm 8:2.

Many people throughout history clearly experienced God at an early age. Below are examples of the ages at which some famous Christians were converted, taken from Roy Zuck's book *Precious in His Sight* (Baker Books, 1996), p. 20:
- Polycarp at the age of 9
- Count Zinzedorf, an 18th-century Moravian missionary, at the age of 4
- Jonathan Edwards at the age of 7
- Richard Baxter at the age of 6
- Spurgeon at the age of 12

In *The Original Vision*, Edward Robinson says that children have a natural capacity for insight, imagination, understanding and knowing about God that does not need to be developed into a higher form.

Sofia Cavalletti, having worked in Rome for 30 years with children from ages 3 to 12 years, argues from her observations that 'all children show a natural attraction to God and what is called the "spontaneous religiousness" of a child' (*The Religious Potential of the Child*, pp. 30–46).

Robert Coles, from his research recorded in *The Spiritual Life of*

Children (HarperCollins, 1992), noted his belief that children show an innate spiritual dimension in their lives.

REFLECTION

- Is spirituality something we are born with?
- Is faith something that grows in us?
- How does spirituality differ from faith?

Read and reflect on Genesis 1:26. What does it mean to be made in God's image? Clearly, this passage does not refer to a physical similarity, because God is spirit. It must, therefore, refer to inner, more intangible qualities. Thus, if we believe that we are made in the image of God, then we have an inborn spirituality—it is part of what we are as created beings.

What is the difference between faith and spirituality? Take two sheets of paper. Head one 'spirituality', the other 'faith'. Think of ideas, images and words that come into your mind when you think of 'spirituality'. Now do the same for 'faith'. Compare your lists. What do you note about them? What are the differences? What are the similarities?

It is crucial to understand the differences between spirituality and faith. If we believe we are made in the image of God, then we must take seriously the idea that everyone—including children—has an inborn spirituality. If we do not acknowledge this, we are in danger of saying that it is only when we are committed Christians that we have a spiritual side. We need to recognize that human beings can be deeply spiritual without having a faith as such.

A definition of spirituality might be 'an innate sensitivity to things beyond and yet part of everyday life'. A definition of faith might be 'the commitment or belief and resulting actions that we put around our spirituality like a framework'.

If faith is the framework that we put around our spirituality, this could include any number of different faith frameworks, for example, Islamic, Buddhist, Hindu, Orthodox and Jewish. Whatever our background, spirituality is something we are born with and we can identify its characteristics.

Think again of the three children mentioned earlier. What signs of spirituality might we perceive them to have? What qualities do they possess by virtue of having been made in God's image?

Consider the following summary of the characteristics of children:
- Open, honest, direct
- In touch with their feelings
- Live in the 'here and now'
- Think in concrete terms
- Perceptive about what adults mean and feel
- Accept things at face value
- Find belief easy and uncomplicated
- Find trust easy if brought up in a trustworthy environment
- Have simple, basic emotional and physical needs

The Children's Spirituality Project based at the University of Nottingham has also carried out research into this area, based on two primary schools. They have attempted to identify what constitutes children's spirituality in a secular culture. A fuller exposition of their findings may be found in the book, *The Spirit of the Child* by David Hay and Rebecca Nye. Broadly, they categorize spirituality under the following three headings:

Awareness-sensing
- awareness of the here and now
- 'tuning': sensitivity to aesthetic experiences (for example, music)
- 'flow': an activity being managed by itself or by some outside influences (for example, the mastering of new skills)

Mystery-sensing
- awe and wonder
- imagination/fantasy

Value-sensing
- delight and despair (that is, strong emotions)
- ultimate goodness (manifested in, for example, security/comforting language of parents)

- relationship
- question of meaning (for example, who am I?)

Now read the extract below from the video *Children in the Way* (NS/GS). What does this poem tell you about the innate spirituality of children?

> *What is a child? It's worthwhile being sure,*
> *For their outlook—not ours—he called mature...*
> *Describe a child, then: Simple? Passive? Gentle?*
> *A widespread view, but not one that's parental!*
> *Yes, partly true—but most sentimental.*
> *Those who've had children know they're pioneers,*
> *Tireless seekers hungry for ideas,*
> *Questioners, ready to learn and solve and find,*
> *Committed, energetic, quick of mind,*
> *They trust, they love, but don't use love or trust*
> *As an excuse to sit, grow dull and rust...*
> *If their imaginations are more clear*
> *Than ours, is it not possible they hear?*
> *More clearly too? Are spiritually quicker*
> *Than many a teacher, youth leader or vicar?*
> *May they not hear the voice of God and shout it,*
> *While we get on quite nicely, thanks, without it?*
> *They may not have the knowledge we possess,*
> *So the Holy Spirit has to shift much less*
> *In terms of intellectual debris*
> *Than perhaps he might with you. Or you.*
> *Or me.*

REFLECTION

Think back to your early memories of God. What was your picture of God as a child? Where did this picture come from? Did you attend church as a child? If so, how were you treated? Can you recall good experiences? Bad experiences? How would you say that your spirituality was enhanced as a child? How was it damaged?

Now think of the ways children can be damaged spiritually. What messages do we give children when we say, for example, 'Big boys don't cry'? Being encouraged to express our feelings can help us grow spiritually.

What message do we give children when we destroy their sense of trust and openness through abuse and insincerity? It is very difficult for a child to understand what it is to trust Jesus if the ability to trust adults has been lost.

What message do we give children when we fail to meet their basic emotional and physical needs? We need to care for children holistically if they are to grow spiritually.

What message do we give children when we make faith too intellectual and complicated, failing to recognize the need to make learning fun and interactive? It is easy to forget that children think differently from adults, especially in the way they respond to God and express their understanding of, and relationship with, him.

What message do we give children when we deaden their imagination and their sense of wonder in so many little ways? We may well ask, whatever happened to childhood?

What message do we give children when the adult world into which they are initiated more often than not destroys their spirituality? Is our own lack of belief spoiling the image of God in us, so that instead of being centred on God we end up being centred on ourselves?

In today's world, spirituality has been damaged in many children by the age of 9. Before spiritual growth can be nurtured, a child's spirituality may need to be repaired. How can we provide a framework to enable faith to grow? First of all, we need to understand how faith grows.

Consider the meaning of 1 Corinthians 13:11 and then think about your own journey of faith. What are the main events in your life that have brought you to where you are now? What sense do you have about where you are moving to? Consider the physical, emotional and spiritual aspects of your faith journey.

Draw a timeline of your journey of faith, mapping out the main events in your life, and then ask yourself the following questions:
- What does your timeline tell you about your own experience of God?
- How does it help you make sense of the times you felt close to God and when you felt far away from God?
- What has been the greatest influence on your growth in faith?
- Who are the people who have helped you most?
- What new things have you discovered about yourself from this journey?

There is no such thing as static faith. The New Testament describes growth as being like 'newborn babies who are thirsty for the pure spiritual milk that will help you grow and be saved' (1 Peter 2:2).

Children may not be able to appreciate discussions about Christian doctrine. It's true that their intellectual capacities are far from developed and they will not be able to make an adult confession of faith. So what sort of faith do they have? As long as we see faith only in terms of what we believe, we won't get very far. In fact, we would then need to exclude some adults as well as children from our definition of faith. We need to go back and ask ourselves what we understand by 'having faith'. An exploration of some faith development theories will help us to address this question.

Definitions of faith

Thomas Groome's definition of faith as 'believing, trusting and doing' is a good place to start. He sets forth his research in his book, *Christian Religious Education* (Harper and Row, 1980). While training as a theologian, he visited a Catholic boys' school three times a week to teach Religious Education. Using the vast knowledge he had, he soon realized that he needed a different approach. He gave the boys a choice. They drew up a list of topics and at the end of the year he saw that he had covered most aspects of the curriculum in a practical way by asking questions like what, why, when, who?

Francis Bridger, in *Children Finding Faith* (SU/CPAS, 2000), takes up Groome's three expressions of faith as an appropriate development aid for children's nurture programmes.

Faith as believing

Faith must involve helping children to build a foundation of understanding in the essential truths of Christianity. For the leader this means providing cognitive tasks for teaching and learning.

Faith as trusting

Faith must involve helping children to build a personal relationship with God as someone dependable and trustworthy. For the leader, this means offering opportunities to experience, reflect, contemplate and enjoy sharing songs, stories, celebrations, worship and family life. All these are tools for building trust.

Faith as doing

Faith must involve enabling children to put into practice a developing faith as they build a relationship with God. For the leader, this means offering opportunities to act, reflect, evaluate and respond in action.

REFLECTION

Think again about the group of children we mentioned earlier. How is their faith reflected in the differing aspects of the 'believing, trusting and doing' model? How would their faith change according to their age, personality and circumstances?

James Fowler and John Westerhoff

James Fowler and John Westerhoff are two names associated with theories of faith development. They identify a number of different stages in the faith journey. To understand their thinking, it is important to note three points:
- Their work is not about the content of faith, but the form of faith.
- Faith is treated like a verb—'faithing'.
- A timescale is put on how faith grows, with attempts to identify stages in that development.

Let us look first at James Fowler. Fowler bases his thinking on the 'cognitive structural' approach to development that we associate with Jean Piaget. Thus he explores how our patterns of thinking and knowing develop in ways which are not directly age-related. He looks at faith not in terms of belief or religion but in terms of how we make sense of and find significance in the world in which we live. For him, faith has to do with knowing, valuing, feeling, understanding, experiencing and interpreting. Thus he sees faith as a universal human activity, because we all attempt to make some sort of meaning of life.

Fowler identifies six stages of faith and suggests that the stages are hierarchical, with each stage building on the preceding stage and no stage omitted. He further suggests that people move through these stages in order, but some may not progress very quickly. Indeed, some may remain in a given stage for most of their lives. His theories are based on an analysis of interviews with several hundred people aged from 4 to old age. Each interview lasted from one to three hours.

Stage 0: *Primal (nursed) faith*
Age 0–4
Faith begins in the carer's arms, in a position of trust.

Stage 1: *Intuitive-Projective (chaotic) faith*
Age 3/4–7/8
A child's thinking is intuitive, immediate, full of powerful unconnected images. Faithing is closely tied in with significant adults.

Stage 2: *Mythic-Literal (ordering) faith*
Age 6/7–11/12
A child's thinking is becoming more ordered and logical. Faithing is tied up with the need for belonging.

Stage 3: *Synthetic-Conventional (conforming) faith*
Ages 11/12–17/18 and many adults
Thinking becomes abstract and reflective. 'Who am I?' becomes important. Faithing has to do with 'how I fit in with others' and there is a strong need to conform.

Stage 4: *Individuative-Reflective (choosing) faith*
Ages 17/18+ and 30s, 40s
Thinking involves choosing and becoming oneself. Faithing has to do with taking responsibility for what one believes.

Stage 5: *Conjunctive (balanced) faith*
Age before 30
Faithing involves remaining true to our own understanding of the truth yet being open to and empathic to others whose truth may be very different from ours.

Stage 6: *Universalizing (selfless) faith*
Age later life/very rare
Faithing involves relinquishing self for the ultimate reality.

Some have criticized Fowler's definition of faith as being too broad. Others have criticized his approach as focusing too heavily on the cognitive and structural aspects of faith at the expense of the affective. Nevertheless, educators and church leaders, as well as academics, have found much to learn in Fowler's theories while recognizing their limitations. Fowler himself stated:

My interest in developing a theory of faith development has been exceedingly practical: how can a thoughtful pastor or educator discern the underlying structure of a parishioner's faith and worldview? We must give attention to what these stage characteristics imply for preaching, counselling, teaching, spiritual direction, or doing organisational work with persons of different or transitional places.
ASTLEY AND FRANCIS, CHRISTIAN PERSPECTIVES ON FAITH DEVELOPMENT (GRACEWING) P. 371.

REFLECTION
What do you think we can learn from Fowler's theories while recognizing their limitations? How can we apply them to our own situation?

Now let us turn to John Westerhoff. Westerhoff comes to the subject of faith development as a Christian educator and practitioner. In many ways, his thinking is more accessible to the lay person. Unlike Fowler, he only identifies four stages in the development of faith, but, in the same way as Fowler, he is looking at the process of faith rather than the content.

Westerhoff reasons that faith develops in community through various stages. At all stages of growth, faith is real; it is not a watered-down faith or just a precursor to faith. In his later work he develops the idea of the three pathways to faith. These are:

- Affiliative: experiencing pathway—a slow and easy route (traditional dimension)
- Illuminate: reflective pathway—a more demanding route (personal dimension)
- Unitise: integrating pathway—a combination of intellectual and intuitive styles (societal dimension)

Westerhoff uses the image of a tree growing to represent faith developing. He sees faith as being like the rings on a tree: we expand from one ring to the next but always have the earlier rings within. A tree in its first year is a complete and whole tree.

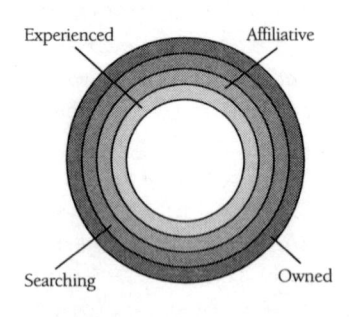

A tree with three rings is not a better tree, but only an expanded tree. In a similar way, one style of faith is not better or greater than another style.

FROM JOHN WESTERHOFF, *BRINGING UP CHILDREN IN THE CHRISTIAN FAITH* (WINSTON PRESS, 1980)

Westerhoff identifies the four stages of faith as follows:

Experienced faith (roughly 0–7/8; Fowler stages 0+1)
Key phrase: 'It's not what you say, it's what you do'. Experienced faith needs an atmosphere of love and security to flourish. Theological words and doctrines are unimportant here. Think of the babies in your crèche. They may be unable to think or articulate faith but they can know they are the object of God's love through the loving care of crèche leaders. It

is important to note that crèches must not be simply places in which babies are left in order that parents may attend worship or other events.

Affiliative faith (roughly 6/7–teens; Fowler stages 2+3)
Key phrase: 'I want to belong'. Affiliative faith needs opportunities for sharing and participation to create a sense of belonging. Stories expressing feelings and religious experiences help to develop that sense of belonging, as members of the church community are observed and copied. There is a strong need to belong and to be involved with that community of faith. How does your church help children (and adults) to feel that they belong?

Searching faith (roughly teens to adulthood; Fowler stages 3+4)
Key phrase: 'What do I believe?' Searching faith encourages the asking of questions and sharing of doubts. Asking questions and expressing doubts is essential to the development of personal faith, replacing faith borrowed from other people. How does your church encourage this type of growth?

Owned faith (most probably adulthood; Fowler stages 4+5)
Key phrase: 'This is what I believe'—an integrated faith. This is the finding of a personal faith and identity. Here faith is secure enough to be open to other points of view and to be enriched and developed by different perspectives. How would you encourage this self-discovery as people continue on their journey of faith?

Some practical implications

If we look at our experiences of faith, no doubt we can see ways in which our own faith and the faith of those around us has moved through various stages. Westerhoff's stages of faith are particularly useful in a church context. For example, we can see how each stage is built on previous stages, just like the expanding rings on a tree. Thus a child needs an experience of trust and love on which to build a sense of belonging at the next stage, and then the freedom to ask questions after that. Without the experience of the early stages, it is difficult for a person to come to the point of a mature faith. It may be seen that this is closely tied in with the development of spirituality in an individual, in that if, for example, basic trust is lacking, then the development of faith is hindered.

Now consider the following:
- If belonging and experience are key ways in which faith is learnt and expressed in childhood, then any ministry among children will need to focus on helping children to experience God in a setting where others are also involved and experiencing God alongside them. If we are too anxious to 'tell' children about God, we could prevent them from enjoying the love and warmth of the Christian community. How do we help children participate fully in the worship life of the church?
- Our teaching and learning programmes should equip children to serve God today. An opportunity for children to hear stories of faith and experience is important. How do we make sure that our teaching is relevant and modelled as real-life experiences that work?
- Faith does not stay the same. What expectations do we give children that faith will develop throughout their lives? How do we encourage children to move on in the faith?
- We need to be sensitive to the fact that our church is a community of people at different stages of faith development as well as at different life stages. Bearing in mind that some children will have developed further than some adults, how can we ensure we do not create divisions with children only by age?
- Strength or weakness does not determine the style of faith at any time. Words like 'experience', 'belonging' and 'searching' describe how faith actually is at different times in our lives. How can we show that we all equally belong to God with no one better than another?
- While we can use faith development theories as models, we must be careful not to impose such theories on human experience. We need to remember that the Holy Spirit can work in our children in surprising ways.

Summary

The whole life of a church community should be to sustain us and move us on. It will be important that children experience belonging to the church community. As they grow, they will need to express their faith in being initiated into the full life of the church.

But such expressions of faith will only be real if we treat children as part of the church community now, and not as outsiders who will one day become full members. Only then will they grow in faith. Therefore, we need to consider how we can lead children in the worshipping community. This important question will be considered in Section Three.

Exercise One

You are drawing up a children's ministry programme. You have a number of children at various stages of faith development. How should you plan your priorities, organize your time and structure things in your group in order to work most effectively with these different stages of faith?

Exercise Two

Reflect on Peter's journey of faith, based on the study below. As you read it, try to identify styles of faith as suggested by Westerhoff. How does this help you understand young people's growth in faith?

Experienced faith: Peter's calling (Matthew 4:18–22)
Peter was well grounded in the Jewish faith from early days. At the time of his call, his experience of faith would have been primarily those concepts that Westerhoff called 'experienced and affiliative faith'. Why was Peter able to respond immediately to the call of Jesus? Maybe it had something to do with the quality of relationships he had experienced and the sense of belonging and trust that had developed over the years. Maybe he saw in Jesus just such a quality of love and acceptance and this somehow resonated with a softness to the Spirit of God that was already in Peter.

Affiliative faith: sending out of the Twelve and the early Church's shared lifestyle (Luke 9:1–10 and Acts 2:42–47)
Key concepts in this stage are a sense of belonging and participation. Faith was being deepened as Peter and the others took risks and stepped out. However, they came back to a supportive community where there was a sharing of the joys as well as the failures.

Searching faith: Peter's denial and subsequent restoration and his wrestling with theological change (John 18:15–18, 25–27; John 21; Acts 10)
When things got tough for Peter and he was faced with standing for what he believed, at first he faltered, as the story of his denial tells us. But Jesus didn't let go easily. He made Peter relive the anguish, but handled the situation so sensitively that Peter was able to move forward in his faith (John 21). As the young Church grew, Peter was faced with the 'problem' of Gentiles too following Christ. This was an enormous challenge to Jewish exclusivity, but, filled with the strength of the Holy Spirit, Peter handled the challenge well.

Owned faith: Faith in the midst of trial (2 Peter 3:3–8)
Later in his life, Peter was able to write with great maturity, clearly illustrating an integrated approach to faith. He was not discouraged by trials, by the prospect of persecution or the possibility of martyrdom.

A final thought

This journey of faith illustrates styles of faith. Obviously, our goal is to get to the point when we can own our faith, but Peter valued all these styles and drew from them all. As a mature believer, he needed to work at a sense of belonging and participation throughout his life. He had to face honestly the difficult questions and situations that living causes us to encounter and that are found within the 'searching' and 'owned faith' areas. He continued to 'crave' for the pure spiritual milk so that he could grow up in salvation (1 Peter 2:2).

Can we identify our faith journey? What light does this give us in our work of helping children and young people to grow in faith?

SECTION THREE

Leading children into worship

The awareness of children's characteristics in their growth in faith and spirituality has led to much rethinking as to how children are included and enabled to develop their worship life within a worshipping community. The aim of this section is to explore ways and suggest fresh ideas on how that relationship between children and their worshipping community can be helped to grow as children are led in worship. To that end, the following questions will be addressed:
- How do we understand worship?
- Is there a theological basis for worshipping together?
- What about the place of worship in the home?
- How can all ages worship together?
- What part can children play in a service of worship?
- What about children's use of charismatic gifts in worship?
- How do we help children engage with the Bible creatively?
- How do we help children learn to pray?

Chapter 9

BELONGING TO A WORSHIPPING COMMUNITY

- To what extent do you think your church is a welcoming place for children?
- What is it like from a child's point of view?
- How does it compare with the church you might have known when you were a child?
- As a starting point, ask some children what they like best about coming to your church worship and what they dislike most.

How do we lead children into worship? In order to answer this question we need to ask some further key questions: for example, what do we mean when we use the word 'worship'? Why should adults and children worship together? How do we work with the different responses of adults and children and what practical help can be given?

What is worship?

Consider the following statements. How do they help you to define worship?
- Worship is what we do when we go to church and especially sing hymns.
- Worship is what we do when we express our feelings to God because we love him.
- Worship is what we do when we receive Holy Communion.
- Worship is what we do when we give ourselves and all that we are to God.

- Worship is what we do when we use all our senses to respond to God in our ordinary lives.
- Worship is what we do when we respond to God in silence.

In one sense, worship is a combination of all of these things. While we associate worship with going to church, our worship is too often dominated by words. As individuals, we are made up of all sorts of parts and senses. Think of the things that shape our lives—what we see, what we feel, what we hear, what we smell, what we touch and think.

We use these senses every day to discover and respond to the world about us and the people we meet. Yet, so often when we come to relate to God through worship, all we seem to do is relate to him in words. As a result, our worship is dominated by thinking activities.

Worship is lived experience. In order for our faith to be real, it needs to be expressed in action. We learn through experience and practice and being involved with people. John Westerhoff makes this observation: 'The Christian way of life is not just ideas to be delivered through instruction but something to be experienced. A process of formation, or behaviour and a way for life based on a particular perception of life and our lives' (*Children: Faith, Formation and Worship*, quoted in *Reformed Liturgy and Music* volume 21, number 1, pp. 13–16).

One Sunday, while I was getting ready for our morning worship service, two little girls appeared at the door of the church with their father. I had previously met Emma and Louise during one of my visits to the local school. Their father began to explain that the two girls had been longing to come to our Sunday club, which was an integral part of morning worship. But they were early. Could he leave them with me? He told them both to be good and not to make a noise.

I gave them some coloured pencils and paper to occupy them while they waited. As the two scribbled away, people coming into church warmly acknowledged them. During the offering, they both came up to the front to give me their drawings. Was this their offering in worship? They sat very happily next to a couple who recognized them, as their daughter had babysat for them when they were younger. When there was an opportunity for volunteers to contribute to our news spot they jumped up and ran to the front. They had no inhibitions at all. This was indeed a very lively service and even when one small boy was sick in the middle of an action song, things carried on at a pace. When it was time for the children to go home, I heard them saying to their father that they had had such fun. In fact, their words were that they had sung, they had listened to stories about God and they had played with some of the grown-ups in church. They could not wait to come back next week, and would ask Mummy to come with them!

When children come into the church for the first time, we need to ask ourselves some questions:
- What do they see?
- How do they know what to do?
- How are they made welcome?
- Do they feel they are coming as guests to an adult's house?
- How do they respond to what is going on?
- How are things explained to them?
- How are they able to contribute to the service?
- Does anyone talk to them at end of the service?
- Will they want to come back?

When adults come into the church for the first time, we need to ask similar questions, but perhaps add some reflections about the profile of the congregation. For example, how many people will be there, and how many members of the congregation are over 12 and how many under 12? If a visitor asked us to explain our church policy on children and worship, what would we say? Within the worship, what reference will be made to the presence of children? What type of songs will be used and to what extent will the children present understand the vocabulary being used?

These questions are of paramount importance when considering whether or not it matters that children are involved in worship.

When I was a child, we rarely came into church to worship with adults. We went to Sunday school but we met in the Sunday school hall. When we did join together for special events, responses varied. As my father was a senior elder in the church, often I would accompany him to an evening service. I met my cousin there and we sat with my grandmother and her friend. For most of the service we played and scribbled and ate sweets. Usually the services were long but generally we were well-behaved and so were almost ignored. My brother, however, constantly disturbed services by running up to my father, who would be leading the worship from the rostrum. He was therefore a source of some embarrassment and irritation to many in the church.

Inevitably children cause different responses in the worship of any church. What would be your response to these comments?
- These children are loved as an important part of our church.
- One day they will be able to contribute and add to our worship.
- That child is such a bother. Why doesn't his family control him?
- Why should these noisy children disturb our worship?
- Can children get anything out of our worship?

To share in the church's worship is to share in the family and the community of faith where its most important beliefs are expressed in words and actions. If we want our children to grow in faith and spirituality, they need to experience relating to God in worship and not just learning about him in an academic way, in their own Sunday learning programmes. Too often the assumption has been that while adults come to church to worship, children come to church to learn. If this is the case, is there a theology of worship that helps us understand that children have a place in the worship? In recent years, concern has been expressed over how our children can take part in worship and for what reasons. What are our expectations? In what ways can young children relate to God and not just learn about him? In what ways does the Holy Spirit help children to know God and empower them for ministry? In what ways can young children worship God despite the fact that the liturgy and symbols of worship may be unrelated to their memories and experiences? And what about children who show signs of restlessness and boredom—how can they worship God together with adults?

Is there a theological basis for worshipping together?

First of all, the theological basis for worshipping together is based on the fact that the good news of the gospel expressed in worship is for everyone. Children need to be involved in worship at an appropriate level, so that the conditions that help them grow in faith will be created. As they worship with adult Christians, they will develop closer relationships, thus strengthening the sense of community in the life of the church.

Secondly, it is biblical. Jesus placed children in the midst of adults; he welcomed and blessed them, saying that the kingdom of God must be received like a child (Mark 10:13–15). He was angry and indignant when he saw his disciples turning away children who wanted to be near him and to be blessed by him. Why did the disciples react like that? Was this typical behaviour of their time and culture—a time when children were considered too insignificant to be with Jesus? Or is that how adults still react today?

Thirdly, worshipping together completes the body. The church would not be complete without children. All generations have gifts and are called to share them with one another. Unless this happens, we are not fully the Church. Children need to worship and we need children in worship for the wholeness of the body of Christ.

Consider the following:

- The church is the body of Christ: God in Christ calls us into unity in the community of the church.

The body of Christ has many different parts, just as any other body does. Some of us are Jews, and others are Gentiles. Some of us are slaves, and others are free. But God's Spirit baptized each of us and made us part of the body of Christ. Now we each drink from that same Spirit.
1 CORINTHIANS 12:12–13

- Age, race, sex and social status do not divide the faith community that God has called into being in Christ: children are part of God's people.

It doesn't matter if you are a Greek or a Jew, or if you are circumcised or not. You may even be a barbarian or a Scythian, and you may be a slave or a free person. Yet Christ is all that matters, and he lives in all of us.
COLOSSIANS 3:11

- The imagery of the body grows under the direction of the head. The parts of the body help each other in the growing. Children bring their

God-given gifts to enrich and build up the church, just as they themselves are nurtured and built up in faith.

Then we will grow in every way and be more like Christ, the head of the body. Christ holds it together and makes all its parts work perfectly, as it grows and becomes strong because of love.
EPHESIANS 4:15–16

- The Jews took seriously the above injunction to share the rich worship life and the teaching of the law of God with their children, both in their homes and in the synagogue. Children were nurtured in the tradition of their Jewish ancestors and that is still true to this day. The first Christians nurtured their children in the faith; at each great revival of the church, there has been renewed emphasis on nurturing children in the faith through their participation in the whole life of the church.

Memorize his laws and tell them to your children over and over again. Talk about them all the time, whether you're at home or walking along the road or going to bed at night, or getting up in the morning.
DEUTERONOMY 6:6–7

When a child is baptized or dedicated as part of being initiated into the life of a church, the church takes responsibility for the nurture of that child. How can we best nurture children in our church? Children may have a good relationship with their children's leaders but they also need to relate to other adults in the church.

Some time ago, my niece Caroline and nephews Andrew and James came to stay with me. As a dutiful aunt, I took them to visit places of interest, including some churches in the area where I was living at the time. As we wandered around one particular church, Caroline, the 7-year-old, said in a very loud whisper, 'Are children allowed in here?'

Children have an instinctive sense of knowing whether or not they are welcome. A primary need of all of us is to feel that we belong to a family, to be part of sharing with others, to know we matter. Just as children learn to speak and develop social skills in their families and find many of their needs supplied in a sense of belonging, so too do children develop in spirituality and faith as they are nurtured and involved in worship in the church family.

If children feel that they are merely tolerated, rather than accepted and loved with joy as members of a church community, they will carry that sense of rejection and alienation into adult life. Then the decision will be taken to leave the church altogether.

Children need to be recognized as having qualities and gifts, which they bring to enhance the whole congregation. They have open, enquiring minds, and are eager to learn, to participate in what everyone else is doing. Worship is often designed only to meet the needs of adults.

Children do not always understand things in the same ways as adults do, but they have their own perceptions, and as they share the life of the church, they are learning to worship as part of the body of the church.

As children gather to say prayers, sing hymns, make offerings, and listen to words in the Bible and liturgy, they join with adults in coming into a creative, nurturing experience. It is here that children engage with other members of the congregation in discovering what it means to be Christian in word and action.

REFLECTION

What are the different responses of children and adults? Everyone acknowledges the difference between adults and children when it comes to worship. Consider the following statement: 'Children may bother adults and adults may restrict children; though they are present for a common event, they do not have a common experience' (*Children in the Worshipping Community*, D. Ng and V. Thomas, Knox, 1981).

Below are some of the things that children contribute to worship. You may be able to add other qualities to the list.
- Awareness of their environment
- Infectious enthusiasm

- Honest reactions
- A physical and emotional response to what they see and hear

Compare these with some of the things adults contribute to worship. You may be able to add other qualities to the list.
- Abilities and attitudes
- Understanding and experience of years
- Ability to apply what is happening in the church to what is happening in the world outside
- Discipline to follow and direct attention
- Ability to see the meaning behind the symbol—the relation of the parts to the whole

From these observations we might conclude that children may bother adults and adults restrict children. But we can help children to learn to worship in many ways. First of all, it is important to use words understood by all ages, and we may need to interpret the meaning of difficult words such as 'confession', 'petition' and 'intercession' by translating them from nouns into verbs. For example, 'confession' means 'we say we are sorry'; 'intercession' means 'we pray for others'. Secondly, we need to give an opportunity for everyone to be involved, whether in Bible reading, helping with the offering, praying, reading or serving at the Eucharist. Thirdly, we need to ensure that people know what is happening and why. Many adults would welcome some explanation about what is happening in our services. For example, what is the significance of liturgical colours? What is the collection used for? What is the meaning of sacraments such as baptism and Holy Communion?

It is helpful to introduce children to responses of worship. For example, the Apostles' Creed, the greeting of peace and the new form of the Lord's Prayer can all be learnt either at home or in a Sunday club. Children will feel at ease in worship when they can share familiar words and affirmations. This helps both children and parents to explore and learn together important aspects of Christian faith and worship.

It is important to talk with children after the service about what has happened and to be positive and helpful, focusing on the interesting and good things experienced without being critical or disparaging. We need to learn to listen to the children's comments carefully and help them to reflect and build upon their experiences and understanding.

Any church needs to decide its attitude towards children as part of their worshipping community. The following statement, 'Ten commandments for the place of children in the church', was put together to help churches address this matter by Stan Stewart in his book, *Going to Church with Children* (JBCE, 1987, page 112). The value of this statement is as much in the process of discussion as in the conclusions reached. Use it as a basis for discussion in your church.

1. You shall love your children. They are not to be kept in cold storage for the church of tomorrow. They have not been sent by the devil to distract you, but by God to enrich you.
2. You shall endeavour to form particular friendships with one or two children who are beyond your own blood family circle—as important for your own spiritual development it is for the children's.
3. You shall encourage your children to worship with your congregation and value their presence—you shall be open to the possibility that God can speak to you through their smiles, their questions, their embraces, their wriggling and their responses.
4. You shall extend to your children a warm, personal and appropriate welcome when they come to worship.
5. You shall allow children to participate in the leadership as frequently as is practical. However, you shall not make an undue fuss over their participation.
6. You shall not allow your children regularly to run riot in worship—by word, deed and spirit encourage in the children a calm and reverent frame of mind and appropriate movements.
7. You shall make much of the festivals of the Christian year and other special occasions.
8. You shall not expect children to be more enthusiastic about your congregational worship than you are. Rather, you shall encourage your children—and refrain from making them feel guilty when, for a while, they tune out.
9. You shall not place undue emphasis on peer groupings and the nuclear family within the life of your congregation. Rather, you

shall teach your children to think of their congregation as the extended family of Jesus.
10. You shall countenance neither organizations nor attitudes which make it difficult for children to worship regularly with their congregation.

Further action

A copy of *The Charter for Children in the Church*, published by the United Reformed Church, can be found on page 217. After reading it, discuss the following questions with your church leaders:
- How has the profile of children's ministry in your church been raised in the past five years?
- What new initiatives have been taken to put children's ministry on the agenda of your church?
- What evidence is there in your church that children are accepted as equal members with adults of your worshipping church community?
- What points would you wish to tackle first as regards leading children into worship as far as the wider church life is concerned?
- What key points would you include in drawing up a charter for children in your church?

Selected bibliography

Children in the Worshipping Community, D. Ng and V. Thomas, Knox, 1981
Going to Church with Children, S. Stewart, JBCE, 1987

Chapter 10

WORSHIP IN THE HOME

This chapter has two aims: first of all, to help leaders give parents a better understanding of how worship and nurture can be part of home life with reference to the biblical model; and secondly, to provide guidelines for parents to devise a strategy in helping children grow to worship in their home.

Write down a definition of what home means to you and follow this with a definition of what worship in the home means to you. Interview three families about the pattern of worship in their home and the impact on the spiritual formation of their children. What picture of home life and worship do you derive from your research?

I learnt to worship in the home. There were six people in our family plus Tiger the cat. We lived next door to my aunt and uncle and grandmother, who loved to tell us endless stories of Evan Roberts and the Welsh Revival. The church we attended regularly each Sunday was an offshoot of that period. We had godly parents who set an example for us as a family in seeing God in all they did. Long before I could speak or read, I was being nurtured in an atmosphere where God was real. Going to church was just one aspect of our growing spirituality and our worship life as a family.

We were helped to recognize God's love in our lives. We were encouraged to give thanks and to ask God to help us in our everyday lives. If we knew we faced a difficult day we would take a Bible verse from the 'promise box', which had a selection of verses, out of context but always positive and encouraging. Having no car, we walked many miles as a family, chatting about many different subjects and aspects about our lives and about God in a natural and spontaneous way. We were helped to respond to God's love, saying grace (but only at special times) and saying prayers at night. We were taught to be kind and to forgive, and when we disagreed we were directed to the plaque in the kitchen, which said, 'I'll not willingly offend nor be easily offended. What's bad I'll try to end and endure what can't be mended'.

We learnt about the wonder of God's creation. As a child I was terrified of thunder and lightning, until one night, when we had a dreadful storm, I remember my father holding me at the window to show me the dazzling lightning against the dark sky. I remember his words assuring me that this was God's creation and so we should thank him for it. We had special family times when we read stories from the Bible. My parents' Bible had been presented to them at their wedding. It was kept on the sideboard in our living-room and was well thumbed by my father. The timeless stories of our family history were retold on regular request. My grandmother, a founding member of the church we attended, used to tell us the story of her father, our great-grandfather Lot, who fell in the dock when drunk and lost an eye as a result! This was frowned upon greatly by my grandmother but she still enjoyed telling us that story over and over again. We were encouraged to read the Bible individually, and especially devoured stories about people of faith such as early missionaries. We looked forward to special family occasions—birthdays, putting up the Christmas decorations in time for our Christmas Eve family ritual of sausage and mash. Some years later, when I made a personal faith commitment at a sixth-form conference led by the Inter Schools Christian Fellowship (now Scripture Union in Schools), I looked back to those early family days where my faith was rooted and nurtured in a home where God and worship were a natural part of the routine of living.

Consider the following extract from in a lecture delivered by John Westerhoff in 1989 to a gathering of Diocesan Advisers on 'Children, worship and learning'. How does this bear out the experiences of worship as described above?

Our worship in church forms us and reforms us as Christ's body so that through our daily lives we can be Christ's presence in the world. In theory our worship is to influence our daily lives and our daily lives to inform our worship. The test of the faithfulness of our worship is the faithfulness of our daily lives.

Worship in the home: a biblical pattern

As far as biblical teaching is concerned, responsibility for nurturing faith in children lies primarily in the home and with the parents. The reality is, in the present culture, that education and nurture have been regarded as a professional occupation with children mostly going outside the home to receive their education. This is a model that churches have copied to a large extent, so that within your church it may be that children's nurture of faith and spiritual formation is seen as a matter for children's leaders, often operating quite independently from the rest of the church structure and home life.

As we saw in Section 1, in biblical times the concept of 'Sunday school' as a place of nurture was unknown. How, then, was the faith in doctrine and practice to be nurtured and transferred on from one generation to another?

Look up the following references: Deuteronomy 4:9–10, 25–26, 37–40; Deuteronomy 6:4–7; Psalm 78:1–4. List the ways in which these passages are useful in helping parents to understand how the home can be a place of nurture and worship for children.

Remembering
Recounting the stories of how God had been faithful to his people in the past was important. Children's minds were to be filled with such stories so that, in time to come, they would be able to pass them on to their children (as in Psalm 78:1–4).

Telling
Teaching about the ethical demands of God and the covenant relationship of which the children were already a part was very important (Deuteronomy 6:6).

Modelling
Memorization was not just for children, but also for adults, who were expected to set an example by making God's laws an integral part of everyday life.

Action

Action was important, providing a powerful sign of the priority of God's commands in family life.

Re-read the first two chapters of Luke's Gospel. Remind yourself of the place of the family and the home in Jesus' early life. Now re-read Ephesians 6:1–4; Colossians 3:20–21 and 1 Timothy 3:4–5. Reflect once more on the allocation of roles in the home to children and parents in the early Christian community.

To be a parent in today's world is often to be anxious and confused. All homes are different. Some families have many children and two parents; some have many adults in the home, some only one. Some eat every meal together, some rarely eat together at all. Some families may be involved in your church life and want to work with you as a leader in nurturing children in the home. When we look at the ways in which home affects the learning and development of children, it is easy to see how spiritual nurture can take place. At the same time, isolated family units may not be able to fulfil the responsibilities for nurture. It is important to note, however, that the Bible always uses the word 'family' to refer to the extended family, and the initiative for the spiritual formation of children was within that extended family, not just the responsibility of the parents.

Strategies for developing worship in the home

Below are some suggested strategies for developing worship in the home.

Nurturing the adults who nurture children

Since the biblical model is for children to receive spiritual nurture first and foremost from their prime carers in their own homes, there is a need for churches today to help and resource Christian parents to carry out their role. If the parents themselves grew up in a home where there was little Christian nurture, this may seem a daunting task to them. For a single mother, talking about God being a father can be difficult, confusing and irrelevant for her children, without a father in the home—and it can be just as difficult where the father is present but has a negative attitude to faith.

Faith is not something we can give to our children. It is a gift from God. But we are called to live faithfully. Parents can share their faith with children through the example of their lives. We can begin talking with children about our faith from their earliest years. We do not need to be theological experts to share our faith. Rather we need to be on our own faith journey, allowing our own relationship with God to be nurtured and showing God's presence in our own lives. John Westerhoff suggests that parents often seem to want something for their children that children themselves do not really want. If parents are really concerned to bring up children in the Christian faith, they will need to stop worrying about their children and start paying more attention to their own faith journey. It is only as we explore what it means to be a Christian that we can share a vital, growing faith with our children.

Understanding that children need faith

Children are learning all the time and gain their values from those closest to them. In the home we can do much to encourage a lively, enquiring approach to the Christian faith as we build close relationships with our children, sharing our faith and ourselves by listening to them and entering into their world. It's natural for children to trust and to have faith in the adults who love and care for them. Our children know far more about faith than we realize. From the beginning of their lives most children can experience the faith as a joyful, exciting lifestyle that helps them meet and cope with all aspects of life.

Most parents are confronted in the early years with the 'why' questions: 'Why does it rain? Why can't I see God? Why did Nanny die?' It's natural for children to ask questions with a spiritual base. They have to find something to believe in, just as adults do, to make sense of their lives. For the child who grows up without any religious structure, life may offer one set of values for home, another for peers and another for school. Religion that touches the whole of life can integrate a child's world. Parents do not always understand that children are capable of a close relationship with God, and have special gifts and insights to offer. Parents are concerned to meet the physical and psychological needs of their children, but spiritual needs are often overlooked. If we do not provide a spiritual framework, we must not be surprised if children turn to other sources.

Talking with children about faith is important, but leading a Christian lifestyle is more important still. Children watch us to see how we live. The learning is two-way: children's lives can touch us, too. A child who has the example of a deep, dependable parent can more easily understand God—who is even more dependable and forgiving. Such unplanned learning in the home is much more powerful than planned Christian education, however good it may be. Perhaps the time has come for the church to hand back the task of sharing faith with children to the primary home and to concentrate on reaching out to children in homes where the Christian faith is not accepted or practised.

This said, it is important to remember that children from a Christian home also need to experience faith outside the family.

Modelling worship: the commitment of parents

Those who have the prime care of children need to take care that their attitude towards church attendance does not convey the message that church is a place to go when there is nothing better to do. Westerhoff reminds parents that they cannot expect the church to nurture their children for them—they have the right only to ask for help with Christian nurture (*Bringing Up Children in the Christian Faith*, J.H. Westerhoff, Harper and Row, 1980).

This kind of openness is very different from telling children what they should believe. If there is a creative relationship between parent and child, the child may go on to ask what the parents themselves believe. If parents listen to their children, opportunities to talk about their own experience of faith will come naturally. Parents can then offer support in their child's choice of friends, their search for values and their problems in school. The situation should never be forced or become too moralistic when children are naughty. If this happens, children will begin to see Christian faith as a negative experience.

Use of language

Words that adults have grown up with may be alien jargon to children. We need to try to understand the spiritual growth of children and how faith stories can be shared. Parents can do much to help children understand what is happening in church life and worship. Children need to be encouraged to share what they do in church and Sunday club. It is important to create space to prepare for going to church: a negative attitude towards worship is created if parents themselves become agitated and tense and are unprepared.

Linking up with others

Many parents struggle with children not wanting to go to church. This reticence may be because children feel unwelcome, or it might be because they are going through a new stage of faith development. In particular, it may be because other attractions, such as sport, are causing a conflict of interest. It is useful to ask a child or young person why he or she does not want to go to church and to explain that going to church is part of the routine of the family. It is essential to be positive and helpful and focus on the interesting and good things experienced, rather than to be critical or disparaging. There comes a point when it is unfair to insist that a child or young person goes to church, but there might be other ways to integrate him or her into the life of the church, such as weekday clubs or home groups.

Guidelines for home worship

Below are five basic guidelines for sharing faith with children from birth through to childhood:
- Tell and retell Bible stories and share stories of faith experience.
- Celebrate faith in everyday life.
- Pray together.
- Listen and talk to each other.
- Be involved in acts of service and witness together.

Christian worship in the home must arise as naturally as possible and not be forced on unwilling children by reluctant parents who regard it as a duty. Christian worship in the home should be both serious and fun. If it is only serious, both parents and children will find it hard to keep the momentum going. If it is only fun, it will lack the depth that should be part of all worship, private or public.

It is important to engage with the Bible on a regular basis. Some families use age-related Bible reading guides with their children, while others follow an ordered lectionary. Whatever material is used, it should serve the needs of all the family, including the children, and never be seen as an end in itself.

The Old Testament passages already mentioned in previous sections of this book provide a pattern for a lifestyle centred on worship, but the Jewish law also sets aside special occasions, which would be marked by family and community activities.

Most Christian denominations celebrate festivals each year and in this way the story of Jesus is retold annually, from the expectation of his birth through the events of the first Easter and on to his ascension and the coming of the Holy Spirit. Other festivals may be interspersed, including harvest, to recognize other aspects of the work of God in relation to us as human beings.

REFLECTION

Take a moment to reflect how the festivals celebrated in your own church help worshipping families to hear the story of Jesus each year. Public worship can be echoed in the home and there are creative but simple ways in which parents may wish to celebrate the story of Jesus each year within the home. For example, every family has traditions and special times. It is good to set aside time to do things together—perhaps to aim at having a special meal together on occasions. Celebrating birthdays and sharing Bible reading, saying grace and sharing family prayers are all opportunities to share faith with children.

Further action

How can the suggested strategy be implemented to help families develop worship in the home? A good starting point would be to focus on a special celebration linked with the church's year, for example, Advent and Christmas. There are many good-quality resources available, providing ideas for special celebrations in the home, such as *The E Book* by Gill Ambrose and *Feast of Faith* by Kevin and Stephanie Parkes (both published by NS/CHP, 2000).

Chapter 11

ALL-AGE WORSHIP

This chapter looks at the questions involved in devising a strategy for introducing all-age worship services in the church. Suggestions for resource material for all-age worship can be found on page 223.

One particular Sunday morning at St Giles, it was a special occasion. We were holding a service of baptism and, as usual, had a portable font set up in front of the church on a table covered with a long lace cloth. Just as I started speaking, it became clear that I had completely lost the attention of the congregation. This was because 2-year-old Anna had made her way to the front of the church and, oblivious to the fact that every eye was on her, was about to pull the cloth that covered the table on which the portable font, containing water, was sitting. Imagine the shared mounting anticipation of an impending disaster!

Seeing what was happening out of the corner of my eye, I moved slowly and reassuringly towards Anna and picked her up in my arms, at the same time continuing to talk to the congregation. Astonished by the attention, Anna gazed up at me and seemed to listen intently as I talked about us all belonging to God and our church. By this stage, the rest of the congregation also seemed to be listening. Nothing I could have planned could have shown more clearly that we all belong to God. It was the very best of all-age worship and it happened by accident.

In the book *A Church for All Ages* by Graystone and Turner (SU, 1993), all-age worship is defined as 'a genuine intergenerational activity with young and old in age and faith worshipping together'. If this is true, how can it be worked out in practice?

First of all, all-age worship isn't adult worship at which children happen to be present. Neither does bringing in a teenage worship band make an adult service suitable for all ages. Secondly, all-age worship is not children's worship at which adults are the audience. Neither does

adding a children's spot in isolation from the rest of the service make an adult service suitable for all ages. In the last all-age worship service you attended, how were the following expressed and experienced?
- Did people welcome each other?
- Were different generations represented?
- Were babies and toddlers catered for?
- Was the whole congregation involved in the worship?
- What was the general attitude and feeling about the service?

Below are ten basic principles of all-age worship.

1. It's not just the lowest common denominator. If the service is aimed at 7-year-olds, everyone will be frustrated. It is important to remember that young children experience the world through their senses, older children can retain facts but still think in concrete terms, and adults can handle complex concepts. Alongside this, people learn in different ways according to their personality type.

2. It's simple. All-age worship does not need to be trivial, but the truths of the gospel at the heart of the Christian faith are simple:
- We can praise God together in celebration of his love for us.
- We can say sorry for wrong thoughts, words and actions.
- We can give thanks to God for his help.
- We can pray for people who are unwell.
- We can listen to the story of what Jesus did for us.

3. It's not childish or embarrassing for adults. All-age worship must be a time where everyone feels welcome and at ease. The aim of getting adults, teenagers and children together is not that adults should pretend to be children. We need to feel that we can be ourselves and not be humiliated by any activity. In an all-age service, young people in particular need to be allowed to find the freedom to be themselves. It may be necessary to provide some time for them to be part of what's going on, and some time for them to be apart from what's going on.

4. It's visual where possible. Nowadays, most people have a very limited concentration span and so visual impact is vital. Previous generations may have been satisfied with murals and stained glass, but today we need to use all the resources available to us, including puppets, visual aids, drama, video, banners, drawings and symbols, flowers and computer-based technology wherever possible.

5. It's interactive. There needs to be interaction between the leader and the congregation. Prayers in which the congregation responds to the leader, sometimes with a repeated line of praise, thanksgiving or request, are tremendously helpful for children.

There also needs to be interaction within the congregation itself. Adults can learn as much from children as children learn from adults. Inviting people to speak to the person sitting next to them—adults and children together—may be an excellent opportunity for learning to take place. This may take some getting used to for people who are new to this form of interaction and it is important to give individuals who feel uneasy the option of sitting quietly rather than being part of a group. Another consideration is to ensure that no one is unintentionally excluded and the congregation is urged to look around to see whether anyone would like to join in group discussions.

6. It's accessible to children. In churches where adults and children are apart at the beginning of the service, but join together toward the end, there is a great opportunity to respond to what has been learnt. Children can show the adult congregation the models they have made, the drama they have prepared or the new songs they have learnt—all presented as their contribution to the shared worship. This feedback should never be presented as a performance. Someone could also explain to the children what the adults have been learning, to give children a sense of the adult life of the church in which they will one day participate. It is important to give attention to liturgies and prayers with long and complicated construction, which create hurdles for children to climb over.

7. It's a mixture of traditional hymns and simple all-age songs of worship. Children need to learn hymns—and so do adults. Adults need to learn contemporary worship songs—and so do children.

8. It's brief. It is important to be conscious of time. It is not only difficult for children to concentrate beyond their natural span of comfort, but it is also hard for the adults who have brought them. Experience suggests that 50 to 55 minutes is an appropriate length for all concerned.

9. It's true to the tradition, but adapted to be appropriate. In some respects, the content of all-age worship is dictated by the tradition to which a church belongs. When all generations are together for a whole service, children need to glimpse everything into which they are growing—including prayers, teaching, baptism and Holy Communion.

10. It's part of the integrated policy of the whole church. Any group is naturally strengthened by joint activities. The church leaders need to show that they own all-age activities as a central part of the church's life and do not place second-best status on intergenerational worship.

The following points can be used when appraising a service of all-age worship:

Did the service...
- express some biblical teaching?
- encourage people to listen to and learn from God?
- encourage people to approach God in praise, intercession, repentance and so on?
- flow from one item to the next?
- allow for different levels of understanding and different spans of concentration?
- involve the participation of people of all ages?
- allow movement?
- enable people to learn and worship by seeing as well as hearing, by doing as well as seeing?
- contain something appropriate for every age?
- help everyone to feel welcome, at ease and accepted regardless of his or her age, marital status, familiarity with church life and so on?

A strategy for all-age worship

Reflect on the suggestions below:

Step One: Communicate. Talk with your minister and church leaders, children's leaders or worship committee and seek their support in exploring the needs of all members of the congregation, including children.

Step Two: Raise awareness. Devise a questionnaire to find out how children and young people respond to worship and share the results with the leaders of the congregation.

Step Three: Talk with families. Spend time with a few families to identify their expectations of all-age worship.

Step Four: Share with the whole church. Keep members of the church informed by writing an article for the parish magazine or church news sheet, or by briefly reporting in a Sunday service.

Step Five: Draw together a planning group of all ages. It is important to involve as many people as possible in your programme, but a committed core is vital if this aspect of the church life is to be effective.

Step Six: Don't rush things. It is important to make small changes at first.

Step Seven: Build on existing patterns. Rather than introducing an additional service, use the existing programme of festivals and special events.

Step Eight: Review regularly. Be prepared to be flexible, to modify your plans and to change direction. Be pastorally responsive and sensitive to those who have difficulty in accepting changes in the pattern of worship.

REFLECTION

What new questions have arisen for you from this section? How has your thinking been changed?

Forward action

What action will you now take as a result of reading this material?

Below is an example of a leaflet produced by one church to raise the profile of all-age worship in the church. How could these ideas help you?

Children in our church

The church is the family of God and there are certainly no age barriers to worship. The Christian gospel is for all ages and stages. If you have been coming to St John's for a while you will notice that we are keen to encourage our children to worship with us. We try, as best we can, to make them feel welcome and part of the worship. We believe this is the kind of attitude that Jesus demonstrated in his early life. He still welcomes children! We want to follow his example.

All Together at 10am

Every Sunday we meet at 10am for worship, all ages together as a Church family. We want children to feel welcome, so below are some suggestions.

If you are a steward, or member of the welcome team, we invite you to involve your children in these tasks.

Little children may become restless at times during the service. Please don't feel embarrassed about this; many of us have been in your position at some time!

And don't stay away because of such disturbances. If you persist in attending, patterns will develop which will gradually make it easier.

If, however, your child's restlessness becomes too difficult for you or disturbs others, feel free to take him/her either to the crèche or Ramblers room. Caring people will be present to help.

Over the years, many parents/carers have discovered ideas for helping their children enjoy the morning worship together. Here are some of them:

- Pack a soft fabric bag with some favourite books or, better still, special books reserved for Sundays. Any toys you bring should of course be quiet ones.
- Encourage the children to understand that prayer time is an opportunity for relating to God.
- Adopt an aunt or uncle or granny! Some members of the congregation would be delighted to help by sitting alongside our children. This reinforces the idea of the family of God and gives you a break!

A positive attitude

As you can see, we are trying to build a creative blend of reverence and freedom. Our aim is to clearly show the children that Jesus welcomes them and so do we. We'd like to feel that our church is one family. Don't forget that children have opportunities to meet in their specific age groups on Sunday as well as through Rainbows, Brownies and Guides during the week. At the same time we want them to discover our worship service 'All Together at 10 am'. As Jesus said: 'Let the children come to me and do not stop them, because the kingdom of God belongs to such as these.'

Joining the church family

At St John's we welcome children into the whole family of God through the special sign of baptism. This simple sacrament declares that God loves and accepts them and we affirm their place within his Church. God declares his love for our children—and for us—even before we have the opportunity or understanding to respond.

Baptism takes place within the normal worship service, but is nevertheless a serious, profound event. The parents, godparents and the wider church family make promises before God on behalf of their children.

We wish therefore not to make such promises lightly, so our clergy take the opportunity to discuss the whole matter carefully and thoroughly with the parents and carers. Sometimes parents decide that they would prefer a special thanksgiving service to celebrate the gift of their child. This service does not involve the making of vows and may be more appropriate for people not ready for public commitment to the Christian faith.

You are always welcome to discuss these matters with any member of the clergy.

Commitment to the church family

The service of confirmation, which follows at a later date, is the logical follow-on from the promises made at baptism. At baptism, promises were made on behalf of the child by parents, godparents and the wider church family. At confirmation, the young adults make their own confession of faith in Christ and accept for themselves all that is involved in belonging to the church. The clergy prepare confirmation candidates by providing a course of instruction.

Celebrating as a church family: Holy Communion

This is such a significant worship experience in our church family life that we should like to ensure that children are prepared in a positive way before each Communion takes place.

We invite children to participate in the Peace and to come to the Communion rail for a blessing while you receive bread and wine for yourselves.

A final word

Several years ago, a working party of the British Council of Churches, in its report *The Child and the Church* (BCC, 1976) said:

The child belongs to his family and, if his family belongs to the Church, so does he... The Church is a necessary agent in his nurture, giving a wider context and greater stimulus than provided by his family... Children are a gift to the Church... The church that does not accept children unconditionally into its fellowship is depriving those children of what is rightfully theirs, but the deprivation such a church suffers is far more grave.

Chapter 12

CHILDREN AND SPIRITUAL GIFTS

The aim of this chapter is to examine the question of children and the use of charismatic gifts and to provide some guidelines for leaders in terms of encouragement, checks and balances.

In the past twenty years, the development of the charismatic movement, with its focus on the gifts of the Holy Spirit, has gradually become widely accepted across the contemporary Christian church. Charismatic gifts include speaking in tongues, interpretation of tongues, prophecy and other gifts described in 1 Corinthians 12:27–30.

Many mainstream denominations now embrace the use of spiritual gifts as part of their regular worship. Until recently, such use has mainly been considered as appropriate only for adults. With the growth, however, of charismatic gatherings such as New Wine and Stoneleigh, which include children's ministry, children too have been encouraged to seek the gifts of the Spirit. Coupled with a growing profile of children as equal members of the church community, this has raised the question of to what extent children's teaching and learning programmes should include material related to the use of spiritual gifts.

It is important to equip children with all they need to develop faith alongside the natural processes of physical and psychological development, and the matter of spiritual gifts needs careful reflection.

Opinions differ greatly on this issue. In this chapter we will consider the matter from varying perspectives and seek to provide some guidelines as to how we may respond to the matter in individual situations.

What rationale is there for children to have spiritual gifts and ministries? To answer this question, let us begin by considering some biblical references to the work of the Holy Spirit in the life of a Christian. What do they tell us about the work of the Holy Spirit in adults and children? Look up the following verses:

John 16:8   John 4:24
John 3:3–8   Acts 1:8
Romans 8:15–17   John 14:16
Romans 8:26

If all Christians receive the Holy Spirit as they receive Christ, does this not mean that they also receive the gifts of the Spirit? If children can receive the gift of salvation, they are surely also capable of receiving gifts of the Spirit. We can agree that all Christians, of whatever age, benefit from the work of the Holy Spirit in their lives. If this is so and the gifts of the Spirit are God's blessing to his people, then this must include children, as they are no less his people.

On the day of Pentecost, the apostle Peter said to the crowd, 'This promise (of the Spirit) is for you and your children' (Acts 2:39). Paul later writes:

All of you are God's children because of your faith in Christ Jesus. And when you were baptized, it was as though you had put on Christ in the same way you put on new clothes. Faith in Christ Jesus is what makes each of you equal with each other, whether you are a Jew or a Greek, a slave or a free person, a man or a woman.
GALATIANS 3:26–28

Francis Bridger acknowledges that there is evidence for the plausibility of children having spiritual gifts and ministries. In examining these arguments from a New Testament perspective, Bridger asks some crucial questions about the nature and purpose of spiritual gifts and whether their character indicates that they were only intended for adults. Further, he sets these questions alongside insights from the study of child development. His thinking can be studied in detail in *Children Finding Faith* (pp. 206–219). In conclusion, while Bridger would cautiously support the use of charismatic gifts by children, he would query the context in which this should happen. Furthermore, he asks whether the gifts should be promoted as normative or, indeed, whether children should be encouraged to receive them as part of their Christian journey. There are other viewpoints that would challenge Bridger's thinking, especially among those who have pioneered charismatic ministry with children and witnessed amazing phenomena in terms of children's experiences of charismatic renewal.

Harry Sprange, writing in *Kingdom Kids* (Christian Focus Publications, 1994), tells the story of children coming to faith during Scotland's revival and experiencing the power of the Holy Spirit in their lives. Sprange describes how children were praying everywhere—'in attics, on the beach, in school, in yards, in fields, in snow, in their hundreds'. He also cites John Whitfield, who wrote, 'On Monday I visited the children in three hospitals in Edinburgh. On Thursday evening I preached to the children of the city with a congregation of 20,000 in the park. It is remarkable that many children are under conviction and everywhere great power and apparent success attend the word preached.' Sprange goes on to quote the writing of John Wesley about children being touched in powerful ways by God: his description of their response is very much like the so-called 'Toronto blessing'. There are many similar accounts of events in Scotland and Ireland in the 19th century.

The current charismatic movement is generally held to have its origins in the 1960s. In the '70s and '80s, charismatic leaders started to emerge, including Ishmael (Ian Smale), a Pentecostal pastor beloved by thousands of children of all ages. Ishmael has played a significant role in furthering the development of charismatic family services in the past twenty years. His charismatic leaders' conferences were well attended, equipping many people for charismatic ministry. Ishmael's main means of communication was through music. His 'Glory Band' included several children who had experienced praise and worship in the Spirit as they sang with him. Ishmael believed that God had something new for children as well as for the rest of the church. He was convinced that part of God's plan was to introduce children to the Holy Spirit where previously they had only known God the Father and God the Son.

Another charismatic leader, Richard Hubbard, spearheaded renewal among families and churches, especially at popular Bible weeks around the country. His book, *Taking Children Seriously* (Kingsway, 1989), contributed greatly to the debate. He focused in particular on the development of children's charismatic ministry through prayer. In praying with children and encouraging them to expect God to work in supernatural ways, Richard Hubbard claimed to have seen medically attested complaints identified by words of knowledge and then corrected through prayer.

It is important to be aware of the vulnerability of children, and we as leaders need to act with great responsibility, but we must not sell children short. Children need a secure church base in which they are given the freedom and the framework to be able to experience the many and varied aspects of what it means to be a Christian.

Alan Price, of Tecknon Trust, is a most energetic and inspired pioneer who worked initially as a Church Army Captain for Anglican Renewal Ministries (ARM). He did much to establish charismatic ministry among children, especially in the Anglican church, as he witnessed increasing evidence of children receiving and manifesting gifts of the Spirit in camps and conferences such as New Wine, Spring Harvest and Stoneleigh. Price saw many children touched by the 'Toronto blessing' both in the UK and abroad. Though he would agree with the apparent evidence of God's work, he was also aware that things were not always what they seemed. In the 1990s, Price noticed a groundswell in the desire to see children truly included in charismatic church ministry. It was at this time that the *Children's Global Prayer Movement* began in the USA as a response to the adult-orientated *AD2000 and Beyond* prayer movement. It aimed to mobilize one million children praying worldwide for other children. In the current revival in South America, children were very much to the fore.

In his book, *Children and Renewal* (Hodder and Stoughton, 1996), Price cites a church in Argentina where the only adult is the pastor. The preachers, intercessors and worship leaders are all under the age of 18, some as young as 6. He also cites another church of 1,000 people in Columbia where over 80 adults received Christ during the course of two morning services and all present experienced the tangible glory of God's presence. The preacher at one service was an 8-year-old boy, and at the other his 11-year-old sister.

Price sees the real debate relating to children receiving gifts of the Spirit as a pastoral matter concerned with practice and nurture, rather than one of discipleship. His argument is that the church has largely denied children the opportunity to grow in their discipleship, being concerned with the *words* of Jesus, rather than the *works* of Jesus. He sees children's ministry as generally a matter of 'teaching the Bible' to children, and 'telling them to be good'. In itself, there is nothing wrong with this, but it is a cerebral, lifeless Christianity. Price observes that many adults are threatened by children's ability to trust Jesus simply, without going through rational processes. He notes that such child-like trust threatens comfort zones, drives people to read their Bibles and invites them to be open to what God is saying and asking of them. Children often challenge our attitudes to spontaneity in worship and other times when God wants to act. Yet, at the same time, they need to learn to appreciate the needs of different parts of the church family. Children need the partnership of adults to pastor them into maturity in Christ, alongside parents and others whose responsibility it is to nurture them. Children's gifts can be received and questioned just as adults' should be. However, God is the prime motivator behind what we are experiencing. Those of us who exercise a charismatic children's ministry do not expect children to become adults simply because they manifest a spiritual gift. They are children at various stages of growth and maturity, and are continually growing in knowledge and understanding. A child does not have to know or understand the principles of physics or electronics before he or she can switch on the video recorder—or even use a computer!

John and Chris Leach also made a lively contribution to charismatic renewal in the Anglican church, especially through their writings, including *And To Your Children* (Monarch, 1994). John Leach stressed the importance of being responsible in the way we work with children and the need to show the qualities necessary to lead children in the gifts of the Spirit, as well as acknowledging the difficulties that there can be for parents and leaders. Because they are young, children do not always understand the full significance of what they are saying or doing—they are simply responding (super)naturally from what is coming to them or from within them. Consider this example from *And To Your Children*.

Paul was toddling happily around the kitchen while Chris was at the sink, when there was a sudden cry of pain. She spun round to see Paul sitting on the floor with blood gushing from his hand and tears stream-ing down his face. Scooping him up, she tried to comfort him and to find out what had happened (we never did) and then ran the tap and put his hand under it. There was a large cut on one finger, and although she has no medical qualifications... Chris knew that this was going to need stitching. So immediately she did what every mother would do in such circumstances: pressed her finger to stop the flow of blood, shouted for Steve, and knelt down on the floor to pray. Steve (then aged about 3 or 4) said something like, 'Dear Lord Jesus, please make Paul's finger better, Amen.' Chris let go, to find that the bleeding had stopped completely, and when she began to clean it up, she was totally unable to find where the cut had been; there wasn't a mark.

Undoubtedly, thousands of children have been blessed and empowered through the work of Ishmael, Richard Hubbard, Alan Price, John and Chris Leach and others in recent years. It cannot be disputed that not only in the UK, but also across the world, God has been doing wonderful work through the lives of children who have experienced the outpouring of the Holy Spirit. Inevitably, such happenings have caused some apprehension and questions are raised, among them concern by some about exposing children to spiritual warfare.

How would you respond to the following concerns?

The right context

What is the right context in which children should be encouraged to seek the gifts of the Spirit? In any mission or conference there is the danger that the spectacular side of renewal may be seen as a substitute for a biblical understanding and experience of God as Father and Son as well as Spirit. At all times it would be important for parents to be aware of what is happening with their children. Also, leaders will know little about the children they meet and have no responsibility for ongoing contact, so it is important that follow-up strategy is in place.

Children are imaginative

The danger of children thinking of supernatural gifts as a version of magic is understandable in the light of the number of works of fiction aimed at children that involve magical powers. Furthermore, it is important to note that the emotional and intellectual framework that helps a mature understanding to take place has yet to be established in the child. Whereas it cannot be denied that the Holy Spirit does give special enlightenment, it is important to be aware of the child's individual stage of development.

Children are vulnerable

It is important to note the emotional vulnerability of children and the consequences of supernatural phenomena. In terms of a developmental point of view, children do not have the necessary mental capabilities and may not be able to control the use of spiritual gifts, or relate a gift to the truth about Christ. Sometimes children do not have the skills or information to respond to some of the things asked of them by adults. The whole church community needs to be sensitive to the danger of laying guilt on children. For example, if they do not receive the gift of tongues when their friends do, they could falsify the experience to make themselves accepted.

Children can be manipulated

The adult leader (you and I) could (unconsciously) encourage the human manifestation of a spiritual gift in a child, because the child wants to please.

REFLECTION

There is much more to be said on this matter. Consider the following checks, balances and means of encouragement for you to use in your church.

Within your own context and understanding of spiritual gifts and ministries:
- What are you doing to encourage children in seeking spiritual gifts?
- What are you doing to encourage the development of gifts?
- What could/should you be doing?

- Who do you need to consult/pray with?
- What steps will you take?
- How will you react if the actual experience of children works out differently from your expectations?

Summary

We cannot deny the wonderful work God is doing in many children's lives through manifestations of the charismatic gifts. We thank God for all that is happening and for the faithful ministry of many charismatic leaders. Alongside this, we are also grateful to people such as Francis Bridger for sounding a note of caution and to Alan Price for reiterating that children need to be equipped with the two-fold commission to 'Go to the people of all nations and make them my disciples. Baptize them in the name of the Father, the Son, and the Holy Spirit, and teach them to do everything I have told you' (Matthew 28:19–20a).

In conclusion, we note Paul's warning to the Corinthian believers that one can have any or all of the gifts, but in the end have nothing of worth (1 Corinthians 13:1–3). Paul teaches that spiritual gifts are a means to an end—the growth of the kingdom of God. It is the character of Jesus Christ, his love in us, that transcends all other gifts.

Forward action

There is much more to be said on this matter. You might like to set up a think tank with your church leaders and children's workers, using the guidelines set out in this chapter as a basis for your discussion and prayers.

Chapter 13

USING THE BIBLE WITH CHILDREN

The Bible is the greatest source book for sharing faith with children as it plays a necessary and crucial role both in helping them to grow in their understanding of the faith and in their development as part of the worship life of their church community. Children do not have the tools, intellectual, emotional or experiential, to understand the Bible. How, then, can we teach the Bible to children, while accepting its essential character as a book written for adults? The aim of this chapter is to assess how we use the Bible with children and how we help them engage with its contents in such a way that it has a lasting influence on their lives.

Think back to your initial contact with the Bible and how that might have affected your attitude to reading the Bible today. How were you taught the Bible?

Now ask two children what they like most about reading the Bible and in what ways it helps them in their daily lives. What do they most dislike about reading the Bible? Typical responses might include:

- It's got strange ideas about God.
- It says nothing to me.
- I just can't understand it.
- It's a book full of kids' stories.

In his book *The Adventure Begins* (Scripture Union/CPAS, 1996), Terry Clutterham stresses that 'adults and children need to bother with the Bible because it brings us face to face with God and invites us to know Christ for ourselves. This encounter can shape our lives in a way that pleases God and contributes towards the vast plan he has for creation.' Such a response would suggest two things. First of all, using the Bible is an activity that is vital for adults and children alike. Secondly, reading and applying the Bible can have a major influence on our lives and we should therefore take it seriously.

Patricia W. Van Ness, in *Transforming Bible Study with Children* (Abingdon, 1991), says:

Only when the Bible becomes a part of your whole being, mind, body emotions, spirit and community does it change the way you perceive, feel and respond. For that reason, once children are old enough, we should encourage them to engage with the Bible text themselves and not to rely on retold Bible stories which are, in themselves, interpretations already.

With these observations in mind, it might be useful to compare the introductions to several children's Bibles. Here are just a selection:
- 'To help him or her begin a lifetime of learning' and 'cultivate in his or her mind a delight in the beauties of His word, the joys of God speaking to us' (*Pre-schoolers Bible*, V. Gilbert Beers, Victor).
- 'The stories follow the order of events, keeping closely to the "one story" which the Bible books relate' (*The Lion Children's Bible*).
- 'To help your child fall in love with the word of God' (*Toddlers Bible*, V. Gilbert Beers, Chariot).
- 'The stories have been specially chosen and related to young readers, and also for their importance in the big story of God to the rescue which the whole Bible tells' (*The Lion First Bible*).

Note that one publisher stresses the importance of fostering a love of the Bible from an early age, while for both the Lion Children's Bibles it is understanding of the meaning that is valued. Considering whether our own response reflects either or both of these concerns may reveal our own attitudes to the Bible and how we ourselves use it.

It is helpful to compare several Bibles written specifically for children and toddlers. What is the stated aim? We can quickly skim the text to see whether the author has fulfilled the aim. What different approaches are used to adapt such a complex compendium of literature for adult readership into a book of stories for children? Is the artwork helpful for a child who is not familiar with the stories? How is Jesus portrayed visually? Is this portrayal helpful for a 5-year-old engaging with a text that she or he is yet unable to read?

It is also helpful to consider the different ways in which adults and children approach the Bible. For example, adults are most likely to approach the Bible through the text and think about what the passage is saying. They can be hostile, neutral, sceptical, analytical, devotional and so on. They may view a whole new piece of information, a new object or a new situation without emotion. Their thinking has been formed by experience and conditioning. Children, on the other hand, approach the Bible at face value. They may identify with the different roles played by characters in stories. They may ask questions, look for new information and respond in new ways. With their limited experience, children tend to approach via their own lives and identify with characters and emotions.

Through the Bible, adults can be nurtured holistically. God's word instructs us, moves us on and guides our actions. God wants the Bible to do the same for children. This means that simply telling stories and teaching about their meaning is not enough. Children need to encounter the stories of the Bible as part of their exploration of who God is and how the Christian faith affects life-skills and experience. We need to bear in mind that we all respond to the Bible according to our stage of faith development.

A helpful three-step model is that we *think* first about what we believe and why. We *feel* next by trusting God as part of our emotional response, and we *do* thirdly by responding with practical action. This model, as described by Thomas Groome, of thinking, feeling and doing (see p. 84) applies to faith development in people of all ages, including children.

We need to help children to engage with the Bible in ways that respect the nature of the Bible, the nature of the child and the nature of the learning process. When we explore the emotional and practical content of the Bible as well as the story, we enable the teaching to be applied to the life of the child, even though that child does not necessarily understand the full meaning of a story. This means that we have to 'get under the skin' of the story ourselves in order to be able to bring it to life in the experience of the child. The question has been debated as to whether children can interpret the Bible for their own situation (a kind of child hermeneutics). The extracts below trace the development in thinking in using the Bible with children over the past fifty years and go some way towards answering this question. Consider each passage. To what extent do these passages indicate there could be a hermeneutics for children?

In *The Bible, a Child's Playground* (Roger and Gertrude Gobbel, SCM Press, 1986), the authors make the following observation on previous attitudes to the Bible:

The dominant and persuasive underlying assumption in the materials was that religion could be taught as a 'body of knowledge to be absorbed by pupils'. The curricular materials were heavily laden with biblical content. Thus the Bible could be regarded primarily as a body of knowledge or a collection of facts and information to be transmitted through the teaching activity. And to remember, recall, and recite the information could be regarded as 'knowing' the Bible.

In Chapter 7, we looked at Ronald Goldman's work in applying Piaget's thinking to the religious thinking of children and young people. We noted too the influence he had on a whole generation of Religious Education teachers. Now we look again at his effect on the use of the Bible with children. In *Readiness for Religion* (Seabury Press, 1965), Goldman argued repeatedly that the Bible is not a children's book: 'The Bible was written by adults for adults.' On examining the responses that children and adolescents gave to questions related to several Bible stories, he concluded that it is 'an impossible task to teach the Bible as such to children much before adolescence', and that it is 'extremely difficult' to translate what the Bible has to say 'to the limited experiences and abilities of children'. Following the Piagetian method of cognitive development, he rightly concluded that children will always interpret the Bible in some literal, concrete manner. It is important to note that he saw those interpretations as 'misunderstandings'.

Goldman observed that attempting to teach children large amounts of the Bible 'may do more damage than good to a child's religious understanding. Too much biblical material given too soon and too frequently may interfere with and be destructive of a child's religious growth.' His concern was that a child's literal, concrete interpretation of a biblical passage would become fixed and final, and they would regard their 'misunderstandings' as the answers or the truths of biblical materials. Having the answer to the passage, the child would have no need to examine or explore it anew, and the 'misunderstanding' would be retained in adulthood. Calling for a 'severe pruning' of biblical content in religious curricular materials for children, he urged that the greater bulk of the Bible be reserved until adolescence, when larger abilities and a wider range of experiences could be brought to an engagement with the Bible. Finally, Goldman concluded that teaching the Bible too early is nothing more than 'a wasteful effort'.

In *Teaching Religion in School* (OUP, 1975), Jean Holm stresses that 'the Bible was certainly an adult book and written for adults. It was never intended by its writers as a quarry of stories for children. Neither did its writers intend odd verses to be taken out of context and used for moral instruction of the young'.

Children do respond effectively and sensitively to biblical stories. They can respond in joy or boredom, in excitement or fear and in happiness or anger. The child who hears the story of Noah and the flood and says of God, 'He's mean. He let all those people die' is responding sensitively. Is that child 'wrong'? In a sense the answer must be 'no'. A story has been presented, and something of the story has caught his imagination. Using the resources at his disposal, he has made his interpretation. Adults may be more pleased with the child who says, 'I like God. He's nice', yet this child is performing the very same task as the first. This child's response is also gross, undifferentiated, and all-encompassing.

In *The Adventure Begins*, Terry Clutterham draws attention to how interpretation changes according to the age of the child. For example, in the parable of the mustard seed (Matthew 13:31–32), a group of children were all asked precisely the same question: 'What is the story about?' Four-year-olds said that it was about Jesus and a seed. Eight-year-olds said it was about birds making their nest, and that it was like life in that when you plant a seed in Jesus you become really good. Twelve-year-olds said that something that starts small gets big and that it was like when we start off loving God and learn to love him more and more. Sixteen-year-olds said that the mustard seed is God's word and can be planted in the heart of any person, however influential or not. From that it grows as the family of God grows and reaches out, and the birds represent the people who come and feed off the word, and multiply the kingdom of God. The word can take a small thing like the mustard plant, like a weak person, and change him or her into some-thing strong like a tree. So even a weak person can reach out—something they wouldn't dream of doing unless they had God's word inside them.

Terry Clutterham summarizes that we should be able to stand back from these interpretations and say, 'Yes, the four-year-olds have got something right and helpful to say, and so have the eight-year-olds, and so have I.' He goes on to say:

If we put all the interpretations together, weeding out those which are clearly not right and cannot be backed up by other parts of Scripture, we have a richness of meaning far beyond what any one person at any one age could offer. Children can understand the Bible, and their interpretation of it should be valued along with our own. We must resist the temptation to ruffle our feathers and act as if they have remained in 'Nowhere worth mentioning'.

In *Transforming Bible Study with Children*, Patricia Van Ness observes:

Studying the Scripture and sharing our faith with and as children would alter the way we 'do' Christian education. The intent of Christian education is to provide faith development and to awaken to consciousness the spiritual awareness of people of all ages and all levels of maturity. That requires an intuitive, affective, right-brained, experiential mode of learning. For a number of years some Christian educators have been writing about the necessity of teaching from this perspective rather than from a school-system way of learning: a cognitive, rational, left-brained linear/logical mode...

Once the story is clear in each child's mind, the leader begins by asking questions. In preparing for a session, begin with the first verse of the passage and write down all the questions you can think of about that verse and each succeeding verse. Before you can lead in this way you have to make the passage your own. You must live in it beyond the purely rational; experience it yourself and decide where it specifically applies to your life. You constantly have to ask yourself, 'In what way am I like that person?' and 'How does that apply to me?' But remember that the insights gained are yours. Although they may determine the direction in which you perceive the passage to be moving, the children and youth may have different perceptions from which you will learn and may force you to shift gears as you lead...

Most of the time the questions will be wondering and feeling questions, like, 'I wonder how Jesus felt when...'; 'I wonder how the disciples or some other person felt when...'; 'I wonder why Jesus or someone else said...'. It is also reassuring to look directly at the child and acknowledge each answer with 'thank you'.

In order to help children engage with the Bible, we need to ask ourselves the following questions as part of our preparation of the passage:
- What sort of writing is it?
- Why was this story written?
- Who wrote it to whom?
- What is the place of this story in relation to the surrounding passages?
- Who are the characters in the story?
- What did they experience?
- How did they feel?
- What did they do?
- What did it mean to the original hearer?
- What does it mean for us today?
- What response should we make?

When we engage with the Bible with children, we need to expect that using the Bible will be a special event. On this point Gobbel makes the following comment:

The Bible is an event in our environment. Like having fun in a playground, which invites us to participate in and with it, to act upon it, and to interact with it... Christian adults have to work at 'playing' with the Bible, of engaging it, of asking questions of it, and of thinking, feeling, wondering and musing about it anew... In their engagements with the Bible, children do and can learn to do what all Christians are to do... Children are to have direct access to biblical content... Without direct engagement with the biblical matter there is no Bible for them to think, feel and wonder about.

Presented with a biblical story, children need the freedom to dare to play with it. They need time enough, their time enough, to explore, to examine, to create their imaginative patterns, to alter them, and even to tear them down and build new ones... They need that freedom and time without adult impositions and constraints.
THE BIBLE, A CHILD'S PLAYGROUND

Engaging with the Bible also means helping children to be open to the Holy Spirit in what may well be a life-changing activity. An encounter with the Bible may invite children to change their minds, their feelings or their attitude to the way they view life and other people. When we explore the Bible with children we need to ask ourselves:
- What new things have been learnt?
- How have feelings or attitudes been changed?
- What forward action might result from this encounter?

We need to help children to express honestly how they feel about what they read and encourage them to think beyond the 'the right answer' by asking:
- Are you sure?
- What makes you say that?
- But don't you think that...? (putting the opposite case)

We need to help children to handle the many different styles of Bible literature, for example, poetry, narrative, wisdom, prophecy, teaching and letters. One way of doing this might be to stimulate their imagination by inviting them to respond as if they were there and imagining how they would have felt.

It is also important to set the Bible passage in its historic, cultural and geographical context. In other words, some vivid imaginative work needs to be done every time we open the Bible.

Finally, it is important to help children build a confidence that helps them tell their own related life stories ('I can think of a time when...') and to learn how to recall and make connections with other Bible passages. We might do this by asking such questions as:
- Is this how you would expect God to act?
- Is this how you imagine God to be?
- Can you think of a story in which God did something similar?
- Does this remind you of anything that has happened in your own life?
- Why do you think God acted/acts in this way?

As we engage children with the Bible in this way, we build a framework of understanding that ensures they accumulate knowledge of God which is relevant to their whole lives.

Godly Play: a contemporary engagement with the Bible

A new method to help children engage with the Bible has been developed as a result of Sofia Cavalletti's work and the worldwide organization she founded in 1963 in Rome called *The Maria Montessori Association for the Religious Formation of the Child*. In the United States this group is represented by an organization called *The Catechesis of the Good Shepherd*. Godly Play was developed and classroom-tested for more than twenty years by Episcopal priest, author and teacher Jerome Berryman, and is increasingly being used in churches of many denominations throughout the United States, Canada and the UK.

Godly Play is a method of telling Bible stories and presenting lessons about church traditions using three-dimensional materials. It invites the listener to enter the story and encourages a connection with personal experience through 'wondering questions' and open-ended response time. After listening to the story, the children decide for themselves how to respond—by learning to re-tell it, by using games, books, maps, or puzzles or by making an art response of their own.

This approach has been warmly welcomed in helping children to engage with the Bible because it invites each participant to be involved at their own level, no matter what their age, stage of development or stage of faith.

Summary

We undervalue children when we simply tell them what we believe the Bible means. Although our own understanding and application will be a valuable part of their learning, the Bible means more than just our understanding. It is only when we allow children to engage with the Bible at their level that lasting lessons will be learnt and a life-shaping love for God's word will be kindled.

Forward action

Below are some suggested guidelines for using the Bible with children.

Train the trainers. Children need help to enjoy an interactive skills-based approach. Adult leaders need to learn how to 'get under the skin' of the Bible. Think creatively of ways adults can be helped to engage with the tools available.

Unlimited access. Make sure child-friendly Bibles are available in church. Encourage children to look at and handle the Bible, regardless of whether or not they can read the text. Help them to see its purpose and value.

Bible reading aids. Encourage children to read the Bible for themselves as a framework and discipline for their own spiritual growth. There is no biblical mandate for insisting that children should read the Bible daily, but we need to encourage them to become used to using the Bible as part of everyday life. The best Bible reading aids are those that enable children to read and apply longer passages, perhaps the same story or psalm over a week, and to reflect on it in different ways. The least useful are those that use single verses or very short passages out of context (and often out of sequence) to illustrate a point the writer wishes to make. When considering which product to use, ask the following questions. What other criteria would you add?
- For what age group is the product intended?
- Are the children encouraged to read or hear Bible text for themselves, and how appropriate is this for the age group?
- How is the Bible used—in larger sections or as short, unrelated passages?
- What are the children actually expected to do and how does this relate to gaining an understanding and applying the meaning of text?
- Is the application to the children's lives true to the meaning of the text being used?
- Is there any room for the children to make their own discoveries about the meaning of the passage or are they always told what it means?

Chapter 14

LEADING CHILDREN INTO PRAYER

In the previous chapter we considered the crucial question of how to engage children with the Bible. Although engaging with the Bible aids personal spiritual growth, this cannot be done in isolation from a genuine encounter with God in prayer. The aim of this chapter is to provide some basic principles as guidelines to help children in their journey of prayer.

Consider these three attitudes to prayer. How do they reflect the experience of children today?

- The meeting had gone on for long enough. The children had enjoyed the session, but were now feeling they wanted to get away. The leader was struggling to gain control in order to lead a closing prayer. 'We're going to stay here till you are quiet!' he thundered. After a series of threats he managed to mumble a prayer, one in which the children had no interest or sense of participation. 'O God, we pray undertake for us...'
- The phrase 'Hands together and eyes closed' and the word 'Amen' were both part of an accepted ritual in my life as a child. I'm not sure we ever listened to the words in between or the words that followed, for we did not even understand them. But we did wait for the word 'Amen', which we thought meant 'You can open your eyes now.'
- When I was a small child I was taught, like most children at the time, to pray to God. I learned words that I sometimes prayed thoughtfully and sometimes rattled off to God who was somewhere up there, but somewhat remote, though I was told he cared for me.

Prayer is a two-way communication with God, bringing us into touch with him at any time as we try to communicate with him and allow him to communicate with us. Prayer is listening to and being aware of God's presence. The proclamation of the good news is the starting point of our prayers, for how can we respond to God without his first having reached out to us?

Principles of prayer

Below are eight prayer principles to help us grow in our own prayer life and understand more fully how we might help children to encounter God in prayer.

1. Know what you believe about prayer

Our own view of prayer and its purpose will greatly influence our conclusions about the place of prayer in a child's life. If prayer has meaning for us as adults, it is more likely to have meaning for the children we teach.

First of all, let's review our own attitude to prayer by considering some common perspectives.

- Prayer is letting God know what's happening in my life.
- Prayer is sharing my life with God for the week ahead.
- Prayer is reporting for duty.
- Prayer is asking God to take action.

Now let's consider some biblical perspectives. Read the following verses:

Ephesians 6:18–19
Philippians 4:6
Colossians 4:2
1 Thessalonians 5:16–18
1 Timothy 2:1–2
James 5:13–14

How do these attitudes to prayer help us in our understanding of our own prayer life?

2. Study a child in prayer

Read the story of Samuel's encounter with God from 1 Samuel 3:1–21, and note the following points:

- God called Samuel. It was all God's initiative and Samuel apparently had no previous direct experience of speaking to God (vv. 6–7). Samuel was in the place of worship at the time of the encounter, being nurtured in faith. He did know about God and had seen and heard much of the religious and spiritual life of the people around him. Children will learn to pray more readily the more they are exposed to worship both in the home and church.
- Samuel responded as a child. He related the experience of 'hearing' God's voice to his everyday world. Like Samuel, children will pray according to their stage of spiritual development and will not suddenly become adult in their behaviour or understanding.
- Samuel needed adult help to understand what was happening and how to respond. Adults provide the support and model for children's own praying, but cannot pray for them. Eli has the wisdom to let Samuel go back and meet God alone, with all the risks of misunderstanding that were involved. Our prayer life expands and grows through inclusion in experiences of faith events, in family, church and community. The example of seeing and hearing adults at prayer both in home and at church can be an important nurturing factor in the process of a child's journey in prayer.

Consider these references, which show how prayer was used on special occasions in the Israelite community.

Exodus 12:21–27
Leviticus 16:29–34
Deuteronomy 6:20–25
Joshua 4:1–7
Nehemiah 8:1–3, 5–12

What was the reason for each occasion and in what ways did children participate?

3. Adopt a biblical model of prayer

If we care about people, we will pray for them, but how do we pray for others? In the example below, Paul prays for the church in Ephesus. Although it is unlikely that he had children particularly in mind, we can use his prayer as a model.

Read Ephesians 3:14–21. We may note the following about Paul's prayer:

- It was a liberating prayer. Paul prayed for the Ephesians to experience God in all his fullness.
- It was a constructive prayer. It affirmed the potential of growth in faith and did not focus on the changes that Paul felt his readers needed to make. He was concerned entirely with their ongoing growth through God's grace.
- It was a prayer of fellowship. The prayer is about our growth in relationships both with God (Father, Son and Spirit) and with each other.

Use this passage as a model to pray for a child in your care. Think of special times to include in your prayer. For example, before birth, on the day of birth, on the child's birthdays, when starting school or moving on to a new school, or at the start of a new term. Beside each event, list suggestions for prayer, including giving thanks, special requests and ways of praying for the child as a member of a family or the community. Also list possible action as a way of expressing your concern. Check your responses against the model in Paul's prayer to the Ephesians. Is your prayer:

- Liberating—a broad prayer, allowing children to be themselves?
- Constructive—concentrating on positive possibilities?
- Affirming relationship—praying not just for child as an individual, but as a person in relation to others, including yourself?

4. Learn from children

The bigger our picture of God, the more we expect of him. Children are often much better than adults at having a big picture of God. When we watch and listen to young children praying, we see immediately that there is a huge difference between their prayers and ours, and they can help us open ourselves to God in a fresh way by reaching a depth of relationship with God far beyond anything we can offer. But we need to listen carefully if we are to help children to pray in a way that responds to their needs and capacities. The main concern must be to help children pray their own prayers rather than teaching them prayers. Our aim is to help children to enter into prayer that helps them relate to God at a deeper level. There is a vast difference between making children pray and praying with children.

REFLECTION

Ask a child to think about a person he or she really likes talking to. How do they communicate? You may like to add further suggestions to the list below:
- Paying a compliment
- Asking a question
- Asking for help
- Sharing worries and concerns
- Saying sorry
- Sharing something that has happened
- Sharing things other people have said

How does this help us to understand how we address God? Follow your thinking by considering the biblical names of God, for example, Wonderful Counsellor, Mighty God, Eternal Father, Prince of Peace. Knowing these names helps us to enter into the spirit of prayer and gives us a rich vocabulary for our praying.

---

5. Develop good practice

The words we use in every situation when we pray with children are important and must relate to their experience, otherwise they will feel

confused and their own experience will be devalued. The concepts we use must match the way children think. Praying with children is about being sensitive to the child's needs rather than about giving instruction. It needs to be:
- Relevant and tuned in to the child's world. Praying with children requires patience on our part. Listening is the best key.
- Inclusive so that the child is actively involved. This might include focusing on something visual rather than keeping the eyes closed.
- Interesting, and experienced as exciting and dynamic. Prayers with an easy-to-remember response are much better than prayers where every word is repeated.

6. Be practical

Here are some practical ideas for praying with children.
- Make a thank you, sorry or please box with a hole through which to post notes.
- Display special pictures of things for which children want to say thank you or to pray for.
- Create a prayer list of people or situations, with a reminder to say a silent prayer.
- Play music to encourage children to dance, clap and sing.
- Write out extracts from psalms and other prayers and use as bookmarks or posters.
- Use sign language to interpret verses from the Psalms.
- Use familiar prayers that have stood the test of time.
- Create a photo gallery of people for whom you are praying as a church.
- Invite single sentences for short, meaningful prayers.
- Use silence. Young children can enjoy silence. This should not be imposed, but come from within. Creating silence helps the child's inner prayer life to grow.
- Use prayers at special occasions as part of worship.
- Share how God has answered prayers, reminding children that the best answer is not always the one that was wanted.
- Use prayers at night when children are often more reflective.
- Be spontaneous: 'Wow! Thank you, God, for your love!'

- Give thanks before meals. Many people reject this as a meaningless, repetitious exercise. A simple way, with everyone holding hands round the table and each one in turn giving thanks, can be a time of joy and blessing.

7. Train adults to help children grow in prayer

Many adults, parents and church members feel they have not the skills to make regular prayer with their children consistently interesting and enjoyable. These are some of the reasons they give:
- The children feel embarrassed about it.
- The children prefer more privacy about their spiritual growth.
- There isn't a convenient slot in the family timetable.

Points to be considered would be to ensure that when we pray with children we address God to fit the child's understanding, we include the child in the prayer and not just as an observer, we watch our use of language, we ensure that prayers are a suitable length and we ground our prayers in the child's world. What other pointers might you add?

As new stages are reached, we need to be able to adapt and introduce new ideas appropriate to children, taking into account their developing skills, their growing knowledge of the world and their own individual personalities. How might we help adults to apply the above points to the following situations?
- A child coming home from school with her painting.
- A parent realizing he has unjustly reprimanded a child for carelessness.
- A family enjoying a walk in the park.
- A child having fallen out with a friend.

8. Be a model of prayer

Children need to hear and see us as leaders engaging with God in prayer. We mustn't be afraid to be spontaneous in our prayers. Acknowledging his greatness in a natural way will encourage awareness of God. We need to be real in our prayers, because children readily sense falsehood. We also need to remember that none of us ever stops learning how to pray. It is an ongoing, ever-growing process.

Summary

We want children to grow up understanding how they can relate to God wherever they are and whatever they are doing, and to share their lives with God whatever time of day or night, not just when they are in church or involved in Sunday activities or the midweek club. We want them to understand that they can pray on all occasions with all kinds of requests, and to know that God hears them and responds as they encounter his living presence.

Further action

What action can we take to ensure that the eight principles of prayer are implemented in our ministry with children?

Further study

Get hold of a copy of *Dreams and Visions* by Jill Fuller (Kevin Mayhew, 1997). This is an excellent manual, providing young people with a foundation for nurturing faith and spirituality based on thoughtful prayer and meditation.

Work through Judith Merrell's practical book, *101 Ideas for Creative Prayers* (Scripture Union, 1995).

SECTION FOUR

Strategies for action

In today's climate, with its changing pattern of lifestyle and day-to-day work experiences, children's ministry in our churches often suffers from lack of continuity and direction. Too frequently, changes are forced on children's groups for many different reasons. Increasingly, leaders are unable to maintain regular commitment to Sunday activities, while greater mobility of families and competition from other activities can mean inconsistent attendance from children. The result is that nurture programmes are disjointed, providing little progression in learning or opportunities to develop relationships between leaders and children.

With changes in leadership and difficulties in recruitment, children have little sense of belonging or commitment to their church group, and adult church members show a lack of interest and concern to support the children's work in their church. It is no wonder that those who are committed leaders are in danger of lacking vision and drive. How can such leaders be helped? My experience is that leaders need to be encouraged to see change as an opportunity for progress and to be enabled to steer a path that lifts the profile of the work in the church community. To that end leaders are needed who can think and plan strategically. An abundance of practical resources are available for planning children's work, but there is much less material relating to strategic action. The aim of this section is to think and plan strategically about how to grow groups, explore learning processes and develop the vision.

Chapter 15

GROWING A GROUP

The aim of this chapter is to discern where we are going with our children's work and to explore the importance of group identity.

First of all, we need to decide what sort of children's ministry we are trying to achieve over, say, a five-year period, and how we get from where we are now to where we hope to be by then. We then need to decide the focus of our children's work at the present time and what our priorities are. We need to select realistic targets, bearing in mind the resources available. What is the overall vision for the church? How is this vision to be reflected in children's work?

Trying to identify our main objectives is a difficult task. In any leadership team there is often disagreement about priorities as each person may feel that he or she knows where the work should be moving. However, agreement over objectives can mean that agreed strategies can be put in place to formulate an action plan.

Below are a number of key points relating to setting up a strategic action plan. Consider how these might apply to your situation.

• Strategic action plan: raising the profile

Key point 1: How child-aware is our church?

What would happen if the children in your church asked if they could help in the worship services, lead prayers and teach the congregation some of the songs they, the children, had learnt in the summer at camp? What would happen if they asked if the Eucharist could be explained in simpler words?

What would happen if the children asked for a duster hockey match with the church leaders at the next church lunch, or stronger orange squash after the morning service? How would the church leaders respond to a request for a stall after church to sell crafts that the children had made for children in Kosovo, or to help with giving out leaflets on the door on a Sunday morning?

In what ways might such requests represent an opportunity to raise the profile of the children's work in the church?

A child awareness check may help us to assess how our church sees the children. Answer the following questions and test your score against the assessments below.

1. How much do most people in your church know about your children's ministry programme?
   (a) A lot (b) Little or nothing
   (c) What children's ministry programme?

2. Does your church offer childcare or children's programmes at major church meetings or church functions?
   (a) Usually (b) Rarely or never
   (c) It depends whether the children are coming

3. Does your church believe that children can teach adults?
   (a) Yes (b) No (c) Only bad habits

4. Does your church involve children warmly and regularly in worship?
   (a) Yes (b) No
   (c) Nobody gets involved warmly or regularly in our worship

5. Does your church ask children their opinion when it comes to considering issues that may affect them, for example, the issue of children and communion?
   (a) Usually (b) Never
   (c) Ask children what they think? No way—they might tell us!

6. Is your church active in community concerns about children's issues, for example, education cuts, domestic violence, child protection?
   (a) Always (b) Sometimes (c) Never

7. Does your church have an adequate pastoral care programme for keeping regular contact with children?
   (a) Yes   (b) No   (c) We don't need to, the police do that for us!

8. Does your church have a key children's representative—adult or child—who is listened to?
   (a) Yes   (b) No
   (c) That depends—we only listen to people who think like us

9. Does your church budget for children's ministry expenses include leadership training and adequate materials and resources?
   (a) Yes   (b) No   (c) What budget?

10. Does your church provide inviting, well-kept facilities for all children's activities?
    (a) Yes   (b) No
    (c) We've been meaning to replace the broken glass in the children's hall for years—the roof is only a problem when it rains!

Scoring

For each (a) score 5 points; for each (b) score 0; for each (c) deduct 5 points. How did you score?

40–50?	You take children seriously, offering care, recognition and encouragement.
20–35?	You could do more to show children that they are valued and recognized.
20 or less?	Either your church doesn't have children or it won't for much longer. What are you going to do about it?

Key point 2: Where do we go from here?

Children are no less important than any other members of the church community. Few churches would actively ignore children, but there are many churches which accept that children belong but do little actively to encourage their young people. Much more could be done if children's work was 'owned' by the whole church.

Key point 3: Bringing in the auditors

An audit can be a useful tool to evaluate where the church is in terms of 'owning' the children's work. It also helps to indicate the way forward in the development of the work. Below is a two-stage consultation process used in the diocese of Leicester as part of the children's and young people's leaders' strategic training course, 'Shaping the Future'. Consider how this may be used to assess the children's ministry in your own church.

The following questions will show to what extent your church already 'owns' its children's work.

1. Why do you wish to contact or involve children in your parish?
2. In what ways does the parish currently reach out to children?
3. How does the parish involve children at the moment?
4. How does the parish show that children's leaders are valued and supported?
5. Do you see children as just being ministered to by one of the church activities or do you see them as members of the whole church?
6. What are the implications of membership for children?
7. How does your church keep in regular contact with children?
8. To what extent does your church budget for children's ministry?
9. What childcare facilities or children's programmes does your church provide at major church meetings or church functions?
10. If you already have a children's programme, in what ways are you satisfied with what you have? What changes are needed?
11. What leadership is available? Are there any potential leaders who might be challenged to become involved?
12. If you are hoping to start a new children's programme, who is available to enable the work to begin or to take it forward?

In the light of your discussion, how would you now evaluate your work with children?
- The way ahead for you is to set up a new work?
- Your children's ministry needs to be restructured?
- The status quo should be maintained?

The following questions can help you to identify a strategy.

1. How can the children's ministry be developed so that it becomes the concern of the whole church, is recognized in terms of leadership, the congregation is kept informed and the relationship between children's ministry and other church activities is developed?
2. How can we get to know the children who live in the neighbourhood? What contact does the church have with children who come to church and those who don't? What does it mean to be a child living in the local area? What can we discover about the social structure, family structure, geographical features, community facilities and leisure activities of our local community?
3. How does the model you envisage for your children's work relate to the overall church structure? What are the outreach and nurture opportunities? What resources are available? Who can help?
4. How can this model be put into practice? Where are the children? How many children are there and what is the age range? What timings would best suit your group?
5. Where will the leaders be drawn from and what are their training needs?

To help further reflection, below is an example of one church's youth and children's strategic action plan. You may wish to consider how this action plan helps you define and evaluate your own strategy. In what ways, if any, would you wish to change the aims and objectives?

Aims

1. To promote a positive image of Christianity.
2. For children and young people to become Christians.
3. For young Christians to develop a living relationship with Christ.
4. For individual team members continually to grow and develop in their relationships with God and in effective ministry.
5. To promote a sense of partnership between parents and children's ministry within the church.

Objectives

1. To promote a positive image of Christianity
   - to promote and develop a high quality programme of teaching and activities
   - for children to have a sense of belonging to the body of Christ
   - for children to know that they are valued members of the church
   - to be real, honest and relevant with the children
   - to be a positive Christian role model
   - to love the children and to relate to them as individuals
   - to promote a culture of fun
   - to have 'family-friendly' events in and out of church
   - to have good publicity
   - to remove barriers, taboos, fears and misunderstandings

2. For children and young people to become Christians
   - to communicate the gospel clearly and relevantly
   - to find out where each individual is in their personal development
   - to pray for and with each child
   - to challenge each child
   - for each child to see God at work in people's lives
   - to share our own experiences and testimonies

3. For young Christians to develop a living relationship with Christ
   - for leaders to demonstrate commitment
   - to establish an authentic lifestyle
   - to nurture the children as disciples
   - for each child to be able to apply the Bible practically to life
   - to develop fruitful worship and prayer
   - for the children to find their place within the body of Christ and to discover their gifts
   - to get young people involved in ministry
   - to provide opportunities for service, giving encouragement and help

4. For individual team members to continually grow and develop in their relationships with God and in effective ministry

- to communicate effectively within the whole team
- to encourage feedback from each other
- to receive criticism constructively
- to learn how to feed back
- for team members to work interdependently
- to develop an environment of encouragement
- to plan regularly and properly
- to pray individually and as a team for the children and young people
- to develop skills and use gifts
- to recognize skills and gifts in each other
- to delegate tasks properly and appropriately
- for team members to be facilitators for each other
- to grow more leaders
- to learn skills, for example, how to lead someone to Christ
- to present the gospel effectively
- to develop friendships with fellow team members

5. To promote a sense of partnership between parents and children's ministry within the church
   - for each team member to give special care and attention to allocated children or young people and their families
   - to involve the church in youth and children's ministry
   - to support and encourage the families of each child

Now consider the process by which this strategy came together.
1. The overall vision was first clarified by team discussion.
2. Each part of the strategy was then broken down into a set of aims, arrived at in discussion as a team. It was felt that if the aims were achieved, then the vision would be attained.
3. In order to assess whether goals were being achieved, the team got together to set measurable objectives. For example, a simple goal was to increase numbers attending. It was important to review each goal at regular intervals so that they could be evaluated and re-set. It was noted that goals were only given as a guide. Failure to achieve them was not necessarily an indication that aims had not been reached. Achieving goals was a great source of encouragement to the team, but

the group was not to be bound by goals. In reviewing how things were going, the team simply asked two questions—'What is going well?' 'What is not going so well?'—with the aims in front of them and an action sheet to note decisions taken as a result of discussions.

Strategic action plan: developing the group

A major factor in developing the group is to decide the appropriate model for the children's work in your given situation with the resources you have available.

Key point 1: Modelling the group

First of all, it is likely that most of the children who come to the group will do so initially with a parent or carer, although increasing numbers of children will attract other children who do not normally attend church. Children need the kind of group where they can feel they belong and are nurtured in their Christian faith, just as parents and adults are helped to fulfil the implications of the promises they made at their children's baptism or thanksgiving. A nurturing group should help to fulfil the biblical picture of nurturing children in a family context.

Secondly, the group needs to be a place of outreach to children in the community. There are many natural opportunities for contact in the community.

Thirdly, the group needs to be a part of the overall church family. For the group to feel part of the wider work of the church, some activities will be needed to bridge the generation gap. It is always a great help if the group is a place where adults, apart from the regular leaders, share their skills with the group. Prayer support and general interest from the church community help to develop a sense of belonging to the wider church.

Key point 2: Organizing the group

There are a number of frameworks that can be used to organize a group, and the best type of framework needs to be considered for individual situations. If existing structures are used as a framework, the main advantage is that some of the thinking has already been done. The provision of ideas and cycle of materials as part of curricular development helps to ensure progression and continuity of overall planning. Disadvantages to consider might include a floating population which could necessitate some flexibility in the teaching programme, bearing in mind that the basis of most structured courses involves dividing children into age groups.

The following considerations might be helpful when organizing a group:
- Do put children in an age group most appropriate for them.
- Watch the age range.
- A crèche is a must, but not just as a baby-minding service.
- Encourage everyone to specialize in specific age groups.
- Consider whether every age group is needed.
- Be prepared to make changes if something is not working.
- Set up a midweek club if there are no children on Sunday.
- Think of having a recruiting policy if there are few adult leaders.

Strategic action plan: a strategy for recruitment

Good leaders are the backbone of the work in any church. But how does a church find such leaders? Below is an action plan to help in setting up a recruitment policy.

Key point 1: Encouraging volunteers

Think about how you yourself were recruited. Did you volunteer? Were you approached personally? Did you feel called? Were you asked if you had any experience working with children? Now think of someone you know who might be thinking about volunteering. This might be someone with no previous experience. Consider the sort of questions he or she might ask. For example:
- Will the children like me?
- Will I be able to control them?
- At what level will I be able to communicate with them?
- What will the other team members expect of me?

- Am I being thrown in at the deep end?
- Who will I turn to when I need help?
- If I miss Sunday services regularly, how will I be nurtured spiritually?
- How will I get more experience?
- How will I get training?
- Will my expenses be met?
- Will I have to do this for ever?

Now imagine that the volunteer is an experienced helper. What sort of questions would he or she ask?
- Will I be stretched?
- Will I have someone watching me all the time?
- Will I have a chance to be involved in the organization and programme planning?
- Is there anyone I can trust for help?
- Will I ever be left alone?
- Why should I do what I am told?

How would you respond to both sets of questions?

Key point 2: Identifying priority tasks

Leaders are recruited to complete a task, but people often refuse to become leaders if that task seems too demanding. It is easier to commit time if the role is clearly defined. Below are some important points that need to be considered by potential volunteers.
- How high a priority is prayer?
- What is the specific gifting of the volunteer? With the under-5s, 7–11s, 11–14s or 14plus? How much experience has the volunteer had? Are they good at teamwork? Would they be willing to 'team teach'?
- What kind of job description is in place to identify the tasks involved in the work, responsibilities and accountability?
- Is it possible to arrange for a potential volunteer to observe a group in action or to shadow one of the leaders for a short period?
- Taking on a new role gives the opportunity to examine priorities. Are there other roles being undertaken that the potential volunteer might need to give up?

- Are there pressures coming from elsewhere? Has the volunteer thought carefully about the time commitment involved in working with children? The children deserve a high level of commitment, as does the leadership team.
- What training opportunities are on offer? How much encouragement is given to attend training events?
- Working with children can provide endless satisfaction. In what ways is teamwork encouraged?
- Is there a commissioning service at the beginning of the year to encourage the full support of the wider church community?

Key point 3: Examining the expectations

There are three expectations of which all potential leaders should be aware. The first is knowledge of what the role entails from a factual point of view. It is important that leaders have a basic understanding of biblical principles and child protection issues and are clear about the role of the church, the family and the children's ministry in helping children to understand the Christian faith.

Secondly, leaders need to have a love for children, a desire to understand them and a willingness to get to know them. A sense of humour and an openness to learning are also of great benefit.

Thirdly, leaders need to be aware of the skills needed to do the work. It is, of course, impossible to have all skills at one's fingertips, but it is important to recognize priorities in increasing experience and expertise and to ensure that training is provided over a period of time.

Key point 4: Designing a job description

A clear job description avoids any misunderstanding of what is expected of a worker, it helps to identify the tasks involved in the work and limits the boundaries of responsibility. The lines of accountability need to be understood and training needs to be included in any job description. It is important to note that the job description should be discussed with prospective volunteers rather than imposing it on them without an opportunity for discussion.

Key point 5: Devising a 'working agreement'

A working agreement can be a helpful way to provide a framework for the job. Points to note in an informal contract might include:
- Time needed to fulfil the role before, during and after each teaching session, including preparation, visitation and team meetings
- Ongoing training
- Duration of agreement
- Reimbursement of expenses
- Support, accountability, annual review
- Integration into church life
- Individual spiritual nurture
- Good practice
- Child protection policy
- Appropriate behaviour with children

Key point 6: Finding leaders

Below are some suggestions to maintain a flow of leaders.
- Ensure that your church leadership and wider church community is aware of the need for leaders.
- Consider an open morning to invite church members to observe what is happening with the children's work.
- Send a letter to home group leaders outlining the ongoing need for leaders.
- Approach potential leaders by personal invitation.
- Consider having a rota in which leaders 'team teach' over blocks of weeks rather than individual days.
- Construct a jigsaw model of your children's work to show how the work extends to other groups and impinges on all aspects of church life from finance to vision building.
- Keep a list of potential leaders in an action file, together with information about each person. This could include a personal profile (age, address, occupation, working hours, family circumstances that may affect availability), their skills, abilities and any specific knowledge

that would be useful in children's programmes, and their leadership experience in the church.

Key point 7: An induction programme

An induction programme gives confidence to volunteers and helps to establish good team relationships. A staged programme is set out below:

Stage 1: Producing an induction handbook

It is helpful to produce some form of booklet as part of the induction programme, to ensure that volunteers have all the necessary information to help them settle into their new role. Consider the suggested contents below. What other material might be included?

- An overview of the church's ministry
- Information about the organizational aspects of the children's programme, for example, expenses, materials and resources
- Information about spiritual encouragement and worship with the team
- Child protection guidelines
- Where to find help when…

Stage 2: Training on the job

Develop a 'four-phase recruiting strategy' for new leaders that involves training on the job. For example:

- **Phase One:** 'I do it.' An existing leader initiates the activity.
- **Phase Two:** 'You do it.' The existing leader invites a potential leader to assist with an activity. Any objections are answered and terms of the recruit's involvement are understood.
- **Phase Three:** 'You do it, I will support you.' The potential leader is given responsibility for the activity. The existing leader allows space for the recruit to experience full leadership by gradually handing over leadership of that activity.
- **Phase Four:** 'You do it, I'll move on.' The potential leader is now acknowledged and commissioned as a new leader. The existing leader moves on to repeat the process with a new activity. A commissioning service at this point would help the new leader to be recognized by the wider church.

Stage 3: Offering affirmation

Interview each new leader to ensure that they understand the tasks they will be committing themselves to. Any questions raised by the volunteer or church leaders can be addressed at this point. Arrange a commissioning service to give assurance to the new leader of the wider church's support. (A sample commissioning service is included in the appendices.)

Strategic action plan: growing leaders

REFLECTION

'I don't remember what I was taught, but I remember some of the people who taught me.' (*Children in the Way*, 1988)

Key point 1: What makes a good leader?

You have been asked to lead a children's group. Try this health check to see if you are up to it!

1. When it's your turn to plan the next meeting do you:
   (a) Start preparing immediately and usually well in advance of the session?
   (b) Put it off until the last possible moment?
   (c) Rarely prepare beforehand?

2. You make a mistake using the overhead projector and your group bursts out laughing. Do you:
   (a) Warn them that this is a serious session and ask them to get on with their work?
   (b) Ignore it and pretend nothing has happened?
   (c) Laugh with them and continue the session?

3. When first asked to help with the group, did you:
   (a) Accept without a second thought because you knew you were suited to this work?
   (b) Spend some time praying and thinking it through with someone who knows you well?
   (c) Accept on the basis of a three-month trial?

4. A child in your group is persistently disruptive. Do you:
   (a) Repeatedly shout at him, eventually sending him out of the room?
   (b) Visit his parents to complain about his behaviour?
   (c) Talk the situation over with other leaders to see if they can help?

5. It's your group's turn to lead the worship next week. Do you:
   (a) Plan the programme carefully and give out tasks to the most suited people?
   (b) Ask the group for suggestions, offering advice when necessary?
   (c) Tell them to get on with it and leave them to it?

6. When you meet members of your group informally outside church, do you:
   (a) Put on the special child-like voice you use at meetings?
   (b) Ignore them?
   (c) Talk to them normally, in the same manner as you would an adult friend?

7. During some group work, someone spills paint all over the collage. Do you:
   (a) Rush over with a cloth and tell the offender what an idiot he is?
   (b) Look up from what you are doing and say that if he does it again you'll pour paint down his neck?
   (c) Send someone to get a cloth and help him salvage something from the mess?

8. As you prepare to leave the meeting, are you:
   (a) Looking forward to seeing your youngsters again?
   (b) Thinking what a real drag it all is?
   (c) Thinking about the other things you have to do today?

9. The leader of the 10- to 13-year-olds calls an outing off because of bad behaviour. Do you:
   (a) Ask the group whether they would like to make a formal complaint?
   (b) Moan and commiserate your group?
   (c) Explain that you would probably have done the same thing in the leader's position?

10. One of the leaders is always late and his group is always noisy. Do you:
    (a) Make remarks about the situation to your own group?
    (b) Get the subject of punctuality and discipline put on the next leaders' meeting agenda?
    (c) Ignore the situation and get on with your own job?

Check your score:
1.	(a) 3	(b) 2	(c) 1
2.	(a) 1	(b) 2	(c) 3
3.	(a) 1	(b) 3	(c) 2
4.	(a) 0	(b) 2	(c) 3
5.	(a) 2	(b) 3	(c) 1
6.	(a) 0	(b) 0	(c) 3
7.	(a) 1	(b) 0	(c) 3
8.	(a) 3	(b) 0	(c) 2
9.	(a) 1	(b) 0	(c) 3
10.	(a) 1	(b) 3	(c) 2

If you scored:
25 or more: you are either a natural born leader or you know how to give the right answers.
16–24: well done, but there's much more to learn!
15 or less: top marks for honesty. Now learn something new!

Key point 2: How does the Bible describe leadership?

Read 1 Timothy 4:1–16. What guidelines does it give to leaders? Note in particular the following points:
Verse 6: The strengthening of leaders through study of the Bible.
Verse 7: The expectations placed on leaders.

Verse 12: The example the leader must show.
Verse 14: The gifts the leader needs to develop under God.

If Paul had written these words to you, would they have:
- encouraged you?
- challenged you?
- excited you?
- concerned you?

Key point 3: What does leadership involve?

Above all, leadership involves commitment to God, to prayer, to the team, to good practice and to the children. Let's look at each of these in turn.

Commitment to God

Do we believe that God has called us to the task? We need to have a sense that God wants us to fulfil this ministry. With any form of responsibility, whether that be leading a children's group, helping at a midweek club or organizing a holiday mission, we need to know that God calls us to the role and that he promises to equip us. In 1 Thessalonians 5:24 we read, 'The one who chose you can be trusted, and he will do this.' We also need to have a sense that God will help us in our role. We may not have all the gifts needed at first but our gifts will grow.

Commitment to prayer

We need to think about our own personal prayer life and try to set targets for prayer.

Commitment to the team

A good team leader needs to help the team to get to know one another and build up relationships. The leader needs to encourage team members to be committed to meeting regularly together for prayer, planning, sharing of joys, problems, ideas and evaluation of the world. They need to be able to help the team to support one another as they learn to listen, to tackle problems jointly and to inspire vision, working out a strategy for fulfilling an agreed vision.

Commitment to good practice
We need to be fully conversant with the material we use with the children and to avoid waiting until Saturday evening to begin preparation. We also need to be aware that we can all benefit from other people's expertise.

Commitment to the children
We need to share an enthusiasm with the children. We need to ensure that our approach is relevant and use variety in the way we interact with them, including fun and a sense of humour. We need to be able to control our group and to know where to turn if we are having problems. We need to be able to communicate in a language that children understand, and evaluate our effectiveness. (See Appendix 2 for a sample evaluation process.)

Secondly, leadership involves self-understanding. This is an important aspect of understanding others. It means knowing ourselves and being aware of our strengths and weaknesses. For example, are we authoritarian and needing to be in control?

Are we extremely indecisive, treading very carefully in order not to hurt anyone? If so, we might be in danger of causing disparity within the group. Are we good at enabling others to take the lead?

Alongside self-understanding, leadership also involves understanding the team we are working within. Romans 12 gives guidance for leading a team. Our team is built up when we meet together to share, pray, learn, grow and train. In this way the team will gain:
- a vision of God's word as we read together
- greater understanding of our work with young people
- loyal, committed leaders
- a more effective programme
- maturity and dynamism in the work
- greater respect for overall leaders
- greater sensitivity to those leading groups

Finally, leadership involves knowing our church, knowing how children's ministry fits into the structures and the overall vision of the church. We need to know how the church intends to help leaders gain confidence and develop their skills. We need to know where to find support and resources, continually striving to find new ways for communications to be improved between the church leaders and children's team.

Strategic action plan: Helping tired leaders

Our leaders are vital to our children's work and need to be nurtured and supported as much as our children. Often they are neglected in the life of our church. Below is a seven-fold plan to help tired leaders.

1. Focus on the eternal God who is the creator and sustainer.

Shout praises to the Lord! He is good to us, and his love never fails. Everyone the Lord has rescued from trouble should praise him, everyone he brought from the east and the west, the north and the south.
PSALM 107:1–3

2. Focus on the living God whose loving purposes are steadfast and faithful, reaching into the most depressing of situations.

You were hungry and thirsty and about to give up. You were in serious trouble, but you prayed to the Lord, and he rescued you. Straight away he brought you to a town.
PSALM 107:5–7

3. Focus on the fact that the experience of exile and alienation, physical, emotional or spiritual, confronts us all. But the way out is to be led by and be vulnerable to God.

Think about the experience of Israel plunged into exile and wandering in a trackless desert. God promised through Abraham that he would provide a land where they could live and serve him. All that the nation held dear—the temple, royal family, palace and Jerusalem itself—was either destroyed or deported in the events of 586BC. Did it seem that the eternal loving God had forsaken his people? But fifty years later, not only did God bring refreshment, he also brought restoration; suffering and despair give way to healing and hope. Ask yourself how it feels to be really thirsty and hungry, and what it is like to be refreshed and filled. As you reflect on this, ask the Holy Spirit to teach, refresh and challenge you.

4. Focus on the active God.

You should praise the Lord for his love and for the wonderful things he does for all of us. To everyone who is thirsty, he gives something to drink.
PSALM 107:8–9

5. Focus on real thankfulness. The exiled people of God gave thanks for their restoration. God kept his promise and saved them.

You may need a new way of seeing how God is working in your life. As we change our ways of seeing, we begin to value both the creator and his creation in a new way. Think about what is happening in your life at this present time. If you feel as if God has abandoned you, think about the experience of his people in the exile. You might like to use Isaiah 49:19–23 as a meditation.

6. Focus on your potential.

You might like to consider going for a walk around the neighbourhood where the children in your group live. Think of individuals who come to mind and ask God to show you what he is doing in their lives and how you can serve him in that relationship. This may help to kindle your vision for your work.

7. Focus on encouraging each other.

Arrange a meeting (not a business meeting) for leaders with as many different groups as possible and with your minister and interested parents. Have a meal and relax together. Talk to each other about what God is doing in your groups. Encourage each other to see God working in ordinary everyday life. Pray together.

REFLECTION

In your work with children, where or in whom do you find it hardest to see God at work? How do you view your work with children—life-changing or mind-numbing? In what ways are you nurturing your own Christian life? Use Psalm 107:9 as a meditation to focus your thinking.

Consider the ways in which the material in this chapter might help you to approach your work from a more strategic perspective.

Forward action

Children are leaders too. How do we train our children as leaders? What gifts can children offer to the Christian community? How do we help them to develop their gifts? For example, what roles can children undertake within a Sunday club or midweek group? What roles can they fill as part of the overall Sunday club? How can they contribute within the context of church worship? What training will be needed to enable children to fulfil such roles?

Chapter 16

A STRATEGY FOR LEARNING

What are the learning methods that you enjoy and that help you learn, or that you find difficult? What influence (if any) did Sunday schools have on your learning experience? How do you think children learn? What are the ways in which they like learning? What sort of learning experience do you as a leader give the children in your church?

If children and young people are to be nurtured in a faith that lasts, there are many questions that need to be asked about the most effective ways in which children learn. The aim of this section is to address some of these questions by providing guidelines for a learning strategy action plan that best helps children in the learning process.

REFLECTION

Think back to your earliest experiences of learning about God. Where did that learning take place? How did that learning take place?

Certainly Sunday school was an important place of learning for me, but while I moved on to full adult commitment, the majority of young people at the time seemed to leave in their later teens, after they had been presented with their 'leaving' Bibles.

What was the problem? In the 1950s and 1960s, Sunday school was considered to be the only place where learning about the Christian faith took place. I believe that what was missing was a link between the learning programme that took place in Sunday school and the opportunity to apply that learning in worship as part of the main church services. Was it true that adults went to church to worship and children went to church to learn?

With the theological explorations of the 1970s, Christian educators began to ask questions about the role of Sunday school within the life of the church community. What was the biblical precedent for learning in the faith community? The biblical picture of learning through the faith community is that everyone was involved in the total life of the church and thus children learned to be people of faith. ('You must be very careful not to forget the things you have seen God do for you. Keep reminding yourselves, and tell your children and grandchildren as well', Deuteronomy 4:9.)

What sort of learning do we find taking place in the following passages? What part did listening, participating, discovering and modelling play in helping the children involved to learn about God? How did the environment aid learning?

Nehemiah 8:10   Matthew 14:13–21
Jeremiah 7:18–19   Matthew 19:13–15

Learning and worshipping within the community of faith was the key to discovering a sense of belonging in that community. Why was it that Sunday schools did not provide such experiences of belonging? As time progressed, arguments about the value of Sunday schools gathered momentum.

As long ago as 1941 Bert Hamilton introduced the idea of 'Family Church'. 'Junior Church' and 'Children in Church' became terms synonymous with a pattern of doing Christian education within the context of the adult church gathered for worship.

In his book *The Rise and Fall of the Sunday School Movement* (NCEC, 1985), Philip Cliff comments that Bert Hamilton's thinking was to be seen not so much as a part of the organizational structure, but more as a way of sharing experiences and insights and a way of giving back to parents the personal care of a child's Christian education. In other words, the whole process of Christian formation was being considered. Here was an opportunity for the church to exercise a community role, a sharing in corporate aspects of being the group in which the experience of worship, fellowship and learning might be formative.

In 1976 the publication of *The Child in the Church* took forward this challenge. The report asked for a radical reassessment of the place of children in the life of the local church, urging a re-examination of practices in nurturing children into full membership of the worshipping community. The report argued strongly that children were a gift to the church and set in the midst of the church by Jesus himself, not as recipients of instruction but as models of discipleship. It would follow, then, that the church that did not 'accept children unconditionally into its fellowship' would be seriously depriving those children and the church itself. There were 18 recommendations suggested towards the improvement of the nurture of children in the church. In terms of the development of the role of the child as part of the whole church community, Recommendations 10 and 11 in particular need to be noted:

We recommend that since children should be more clearly seen to be part of the worshipping community churches should give careful consideration to times, places and patterns of worship in order to effect the appropriate integration of children and adults.
RECOMMENDATION 10: WORSHIP INTEGRATION

We recommend that gatherings of the local church for worship should be modified so that greater opportunity is created for the participation of children in ways appropriate to them and to the liturgy.
RECOMMENDATION 11: WORSHIP PARTICIPATION

The impact of this report was so strong that it was felt necessary to produce a further report, *Understanding Christian Nurture*, published in 1981, to take the thinking of *The Child in the Church* further. In a time of rapid cultural change, this report stressed the need for adult Christians to accept that ways of expressing Christian thought and feeling which they had found meaningful and satisfactory might not be equally meaningful and satisfactory for their children. To be effective, Christian nurture meant learning from each other. One of the marks of Christian maturity was a willingness to accept each other in spite of differences of culture. If there was in Christ 'neither Jew nor Greek, bond nor free, male nor female', then there was in him neither young nor old. If there was a generation gap in our society, the Church ought to be one of the places where that gap was most readily bridged.

A further contribution to the debate was made by John Sutcliffe in *Learning and Teaching Together* (Chester House Publications, 1980). He made some searching comments about the classifying and clarifying of aims, and closely scrutinized popular assumptions linked with styles of learning as seen in the traditional Sunday schools. His argument was that Sunday school as an inheritance was no longer needed. What was needed were churches where children would both learn about the faith and participate in it. This point was further stressed by Rosemary Nixon in her research, *Who's the Greatest?* (NS, 1985):

The decline of the Sunday school is probably a blessing in disguise! Instead of bemoaning its demise, we must have the courage of its founders and consider what God is saying to the Church... (This) is an opportunity to think afresh about what constitutes church membership; what is important in weekly worship and what is at the heart of the Christian tradition. Fresh theological and education insights can help us in this urgent task to which clergy, Sunday school teachers and congregations alike must address themselves in order to end the isolation of the Sunday school and the corresponding social and spiritual diminishment of the Church.

Is Sunday school the wrong model of learning? This was a particular concern of *Children in the Way*, produced in 1988. Recognizing the radical changes in society as far as children were concerned, a survey conducted in 25 dioceses of the Church of England looked at models for Christian education and suggested ways forward in which adults and children could share the journey of faith as new strategies for learning were adopted.

The image of the Church as a pilgrim community adds new dimensions, which may be helpful. While the school model can all too easily be interpreted as teacher and taught, and the family model may feel too restricted, the pilgrim community comprises a band of people all sharing in and learning from common experience.

In the following year, a collection of essays, *'Issues in the Christian Initiation of Children*, edited by Brown and Sokal (LTP, 1989), was published. It included an essay by John Westerhoff entitled 'The formative nature of liturgy', in which he described the processes essential to Christian growth under three headings—formation, education and instruction.

Instruction helps persons to acquire knowledge and skills useful for responsible personal and communal Christian life in church and society. For example, through ability to comprehend and interpret its meaning for daily life and techniques such as meditation. Similarly, through instructional processes persons acquire a knowledge of Christian theology and ethics as well as the ability to think theologically and to make moral decisions. Instruction or technical learning informs but requires the ability to engage in rational processes of cognition that developmentally are not possible until early adolescence. As such, it is therefore neither a necessary nor appropriate activity for children nor others who are unable to engage in formal operational cognitive processes; nevertheless, foundational knowledge such as the gospel narrative and basic skills such as oral prayer can be acquired by children through participation in formational activities.

Education helps persons develop and actualize human potential and achieve individuation, makes possible the reformation of personal and communal faith and life, and enables persons to relate Christian faith to daily life and work. As such, Christian education is best understood as critical reflection on experience in the light of Christian faith and life. For example, through reflection on cultic life and other aspects of life within a community of Christian faith, the church can reform its cultic life and thereby become a more faithful community. Education or humanizing learning re-forms, which requires a knowledge of Christian faith and life not possible until adolescence. Therefore, it is neither a necessary or appropriate activity for children; nevertheless, the process of reflection on experience can be acquired by children through participation in formational activities.

Christian formation, which inducts persons into the body of Christ, is intended to shape and sustain persons' faith or perception of all life, their lives, their character, their identity, their behavioural dispositions, their consciousness or attitudes and values. Formation is a natural activity known as enculturation, socialization about which we are intentional. Christian formation or nurture involves the experience of Christian faith and life, and while it is a lifelong activity, it is especially necessary and appropriate for children. Too long have catechists placed emphasis on instruction of children while neglecting both the formation of children and the education of youth and adults. (pp. 146–147)

Below is an extract from the *Baptist Times*, 28 January 1993. How might we respond to these comments?

Eleven reasons to abolish Sunday schools

1. They distort the worshipping community.
   The active have gone to their activities, the passive remain.
2. They segregate the church.
   Who else likes to sit at the front?
3. They impoverish worship.
   When children leave the service, with them goes some of the most valuable resources.
4. They inhibit Christian growth.
   The greatest obstacle in taking part in adult church life is often the gulf between the adult and children's worship.
5. They give the wrong message to children.
   Children sent by their parents will grow out of this as they grow out of school.
6. They give the wrong message to the community.
   Church and the Christian faith are primarily for children.
7. They divert churches' investment in the future.
   Children are not the church of the future but the church of today.
8. They inhibit church growth.
   Because we have downgraded teaching into a children's activity, we make it very hard for unchurched adults to become familiar with the faith.
9. They enshrine an untheological view of children.
   Jesus used children as models of the kingdom, but we seem to use children as empty vessels to be filled with knowledge with their elders.
10. They are anti-evangelistic.
    Children never stand next to a believer moved to tears. Do children think faith is something to learn rather than to be lived?
11. No one person should be designated as a learner or teacher. We are all both.

New Directions in Children's Ministry, a consultation that took place at London Bible College in 1995, continued this debate. The consultation brought together 90 delegates from diverse backgrounds with a common ministry to children. The aim of the consultation was to examine current issues, to set an agenda for action and to help shape a vision for the future direction of children's ministry. Key issues included revising again the question of the inclusion of children within the worshipping and learning community of the church. To assess progress in this debate, consider the agenda for action to be found on pages 217–218.

A strategy for learning

Key point 1: Recognize what is involved in learning

What is the chief task of any church? How does the church fulfil its primary learning task by helping its members share and shape their faith? Let's look again at Westerhoff's words as quoted above.

Formation is a natural activity known as enculturation, socialization about which we are intentional. Christian formation or nurture involves the experiences of Christian faith and life, and while it is a lifelong activity, it is especially necessary and appropriate for children.

From the outset we need to acknowledge that learning is much more than instruction, but a shaping of a faith.

REFLECTION

Think back to two new things you learnt recently. Did you learn in a planned and formally experienced way, such as by reading a book? Or was it through unplanned, informal experiences, for instance, listening to someone's opinion, or noting the interaction of individuals, the manner in which someone includes or excludes other people?

Key point 2: Recognize patterns in learning

It is possible to identify a pattern where effective learning takes place. Below is an example of such a learning pattern.
- Experience: why did that work?
- Reflection: how can I do that?
- Concept formation: that's a new idea.
- Action: let's try it out.

Think of the many everyday life experiences children encounter, and how each of their senses—touch, taste, smell, hearing and sight—provides a means of interpreting the experiences of that world around them. Consider how each experience builds on previous experiences, forming a background for children to reflect on as they assess new information. Think of the new learning acquired by children actively participating in their own learning process.

Key point 3: Recognize differences in learning

Trends in the past years have led to some key investigations into the use of different learning styles. Think again of the methods of learning you like best. What do you like least? We learn in different ways—exploring places, listening to someone, watching children play, arguing with a friend, reading, listening to a sermon and so on.

Consider a group of children with whom you have worked. Within that group there are likely to be at least four different learning preferences.

Group A: Learns best by working in groups. These are the children who learn through interaction with peers. They like talking things over and sharing together. If we were to insist that any child in this group were to listen for more than a few minutes, we would soon discover that little learning was accomplished.

Group B: Learns best by listening. This would be the type of group that likes learning in a traditional classroom setting. These children would enjoy listening to you conversing with them.

Group C: Learns best by being involved. This group would be those who are task-centred learners. For example, they look forward to taking home their activity leaflets to show what they are learning about God.

Group D: Learns best by being creative. This group likes working on projects. We may need to create games to help their learning process. A helpful way to do this might be to think of a game they could devise to help them learn the Bible.

How would you develop the learning experiences in these groups, bearing in mind their preferred learning styles?

Key point 4: Recognize what needs to be learnt

Here is a suggested list of the things children need to learn about. You might want to add to this.
- Themselves
- Other people
- The world in which they live
- God
- Jesus
- The church
- The Holy Spirit

How do we help children to learn these things in the church and in children's groups?

Key point 5: Recognize how 'belonging' helps learning

John Westerhoff describes Christian learning as 'enculturation' into the Christian community. Westerhoff emphasizes that the child can appreciate, through belonging to a worshipping community, the values of the Bible and how he or she may be part of those values and that community. A sense of belonging comes from a developing relationship, and learning stems from having relationships. The network of a child's relationships includes the family. In what ways might we involve parents in our learning programmes? Christian learning becomes more effective when it is linked into other activities in the life of the church. How do we involve our church leaders and what opportunities could be created for all ages to learn together?

Key point 6: Recognize how tradition helps learning

Celebration is a significant part of normal life, yet is often underrated in the church. The Old Testament depicts family life with regular celebrations of significant religious events, which involve all ages together, remembering and retelling stories that were an integral part of life, rich in meaning. Children learn much from the practice of festivals and special events of the Christian year. The story of the faith can be repeated at intervals, becoming part of the shared life that bonds the sense of belonging in the community.

REFLECTION
How can we use festivals as part of the learning process?

Key point 7: Recognize good practice in learning

Much material has been produced on the practical aspects of devising a learning programme, and the following points are by no means exhaustive.

Developing communication skills

Children take in 10 per cent of what they hear: 'I hear and I forget.'
Children take in 50 per cent of what they see: 'I see and I understand.'
Children take in 90 per cent of what they do: 'I do and I remember.'

Which style of programme might encourage learning that lasts?
- Smooth-running
- Keeping to time at all costs
- Hurriedly prepared
- No fixed line of responsibility

- Disintegrated planning
- Everybody helping
- Same each week
- Integrated planning

Long-term programme planning

Below are some suggestions to facilitate a plan of action.
1. Define the vision, goals and aims.
2. Set realistic targets for the leaders and the children.
3. Plan ahead.
4. Use biblical topics, not just Bible stories.
5. Make sure all the leaders are working in the same direction!
6. Include an evaluation (a suggested outline is included in Appendix 2.)

Week-by-week programme planning

1. Define your vision, goals and aims.
2. Pray for and expect results.
3. Plan in adequate preparation time during the week.
4. Have an understandable aim for the day.
5. Be clear about the objectives: are we training the children, or just telling them stories?
6. Ask yourself: have I achieved what I set out to do?

Qualities of a good programme

- Concrete images are preferable to abstract concepts. For example, in the parable of the lost sheep in Luke 15, the abstract concept is that God is love. The phrase 'God is love' only occurs twice in the Bible, but there are numerous pictures and stories expressing God's love.
- Use plenty of humour. The Bible is full of humour—for example, a parent giving a child a stone or snake in Matthew 7:9–10. The parables are often larger than life—for example, the man owing 10,000 talents.
- Make sure the teaching relates to the world of the child. Jesus always used pictures that helped people to identify his teaching with everyday life—for example, farmers and seeds, fruit trees and sheep.
- Make it memorable! Over half of Jesus' teaching in the Gospels is in story form. Children forget teaching points but remember stories. You

can repeat the same points every week, but you can't tell the same story twice!
- Include an element of surprise. An interesting session will include an element that takes people by surprise. As an example, look for the element of surprise in the parable of the good Samaritan or the father and two sons.
- Make it stimulating. Get the children involved in the teaching, looking up the Bible passages, participating in the story and prayers, contributing to the activities and so on.

A weekly session

In planning any session, the aim of the session is your link factor.
1. The starting point needs to be within the child's own experience.
2. Bridge-building activities: including games, interactive story and so on.
3. Fact gathering: including the Bible teaching, learning material, stories, memory verse and so on.
4. Action: apply the teaching, perhaps using puppets, drama, story, hot spot and so on.
5. Worship and spirituality: including music and prayer.
6. Reinforcement of teaching: using games, craft, puppets, hot spot, summary and unrelated fun activities.

A practical example

You have a group of 16 children between the ages of 5 and 10. Generally you remain in church for the first 20 minutes and then have 40 minutes for children's club. You have one large hall and one smaller area where coffee will be served at the end of the service. Using Luke 17:11–19, the story of the ten lepers, design a session as follows:
1. Base the teaching on the theme that it is good to give thanks to God and others.
2. List possible activities including story 'research', quiz, crafts, worship, drama and artwork.
3. Select appropriate activities that link into the theme, the age group, the time available and the needs of the group.

4. Design the programme to include different interests with clear start and finish points. Ensure that the theme is reinforced throughout.
5. Plan the details. Collect materials together, prepare visuals, allocate jobs.
6. Consider how you will evaluate the programme.

Key point 8: Recognize the importance of modelling

Adult leaders are a powerful role model for children, just as Jesus' life was a learning example for his followers. By his everyday actions of love, his wisdom and his willingness to heal, he showed a learning model of deep love for all. For children everyday actions teach volumes. Children will constantly match what is said with what is done. However contemporary our learning resources may be, they will be meaningless if the children do not see truth lived out by adults in the church. This is a major part of the strategies for learning. As Proverbs says, 'Teach your children right from wrong, and when they are grown they will still do right' (Proverbs 22:6).

Further action

What would you expect a 10-year-old in your group to have learnt about the foundations of the Christian faith? What would you expect that young person to learn over the course of the next year? The next three years? In what ways could we ensure the process of learning is encouraged within our church community? What strategy action plan could we devise to ensure that learning takes place?

Chapter 17

REACHING CHILDREN ON THE FRINGE

For many years, I had been involved in programmes of evangelism and outreach with people of all ages and backgrounds. Then I became vicar of a village church largely consisting of 'fringe' people who, as they saw it, were committed to the church but only attended occasionally. The fact that parents came intermittently meant that children too were no longer regularly present at Sunday activities. My challenge was not so much coping with declining numbers of children as with the fact that there was no children's work in the church at all.

I found this difficult to understand. The village had a population of 4,000, a flourishing church school and three playgroups—not to mention uniformed organizations. I realized that many of the children had some vague contact with the church. Furthermore, baptisms were prolific, so contacts here could be useful. But on Sundays there were few children in church. Children who were coming were often brought by parents who were themselves 'returning' to church because at some point in their background they had attended Sunday school. How could I draw in 'the fringe' to be more committed in their personal faith as well as to the life of the church? Clearly some of the conventional methods of evangelism were inadequate. A new strategy was needed to reach children on the fringe.

The aim of this chapter is to suggest how such a strategy can be devised to meet the challenges of today's church.

Think of people of all ages who are involved in the life of your church, either because they have some contact through friends and relatives in the church, or because they have children who attend a weekly club linked with the church. Think of the children who have family and friends who come occasionally to events. Who are they? Why do they come? Would you describe them as fringe members? How do they view their sense of commitment to the church? How do we help children and their families grow in commitment to God and to the life of the church community?

Think of the families and children in your community who never come to church. Why don't they come? What can we do to build up links and reach out with a programme of evangelism to such people? What evangelism strategy would be appropriate within the community?

The concerns many of us struggle with have been reflected nationally, especially in three reports published in the past ten years. The first was *All God's Children?* published in 1991. The rapid decline in children attending church was highlighted in this report, which came as a response to the debate resulting in the General Synod report, *Children in the Way*. Clearly, there was a crisis looming with regard to the number of children regularly in contact with a place of worship. A request was made for Synod to note the low percentage of children in touch with the churches (15 per cent) and to give further attention to the types of children's evangelism needed at this time. A number of key questions were explored regarding how and why children on the fringe of church life could be reached. Children needed to be taught about God, to grow as part of a church community and to be re-established in their rightful place as part of God's family. Conclusions were listed as follows:

- God loves them as a good heavenly father.
- They need to know they are worth something, for Christ died for them.
- There is a plan for them and their lives.
- They need to experience love from others.
- They need to be accepted unconditionally.
- They need to enjoy childhood.
- They need to have a place of safety.
- They need be aware of God's action in the world through the Holy Spirit.
- They need to see beyond materialism.
- They need to know that they are equal partners with adults in the life of the Church.

All God's Children? was a key text in redefining methods of reaching children outside the church and the reasons for doing so. Essentially the report argued that children's evangelism should not be judged in terms of instant results with a narrow concern for church recruitment, but rather as a 'kingdom' activity. Further, reaching out to children in this rapidly changing society meant recognizing that there were certain assumptions that could no longer be made as far as children's ministry was concerned. For instance, parental support could not be guaranteed, nor any previous knowledge of the Bible, nor even that those children would want to come to activities on Sundays. Certainly, evangelism amongst children was in crisis. How would the church respond?

A summary of recommendations as set out in the report is listed below. To what extent has the church responded to these recommendations? How do they help us as we shape a strategy to reach children on the fringe in our own individual situations?

- The church must reach out to children apart from their parents where necessary, as well as to whole families.
- Only 13 per cent of children are in contact with a church and only 2–5 per cent are likely to become adult members.
- Every child should be given the benefit of being part of a family of people experiencing the presence of Christ in and through others.
- An attractive situation needs to be provided to which children can invite their friends without embarrassment.
- An overuse of family worship has meant little contact with children whose parents refuse to come to church.
- Churches should give strong support to Christian teachers and children in school.
- The Church has continued to use a school-based model which is inappropriate for learning about Christ, and has bored children by not keeping abreast of new teaching methods.
- It should be acknowledged that children can and do make clear-cut steps forward in personal faith, but children should not be put under pressure to respond to the gospel.
- Lasting impressions need to be planted in children, which may result in long-term faith and commitment and not necessarily immediate response.
- Each church must have a continuing pastoral strategy for children's work—high on the Parochial Church Council agenda—and pay the price in terms of money, time, talents and stamina of church members.

- Help and guidelines are needed for those who have the opportunity to present and model the Christian faith in schools.
- Forms of evangelism appropriate in attracting children with no support from their parents need to be explored.

The second report was *Unfinished Business*, produced in 1995 by the Consultative Group on Ministry among Children. This report perceived that the issue did not rest with *All God's Children?* If 87 per cent of children never went to church, how could they be reached? The focus of outreach was shifting from the child in the church to the child in society, the community, the home and school. New concepts, such as the erosion of childhood, the 'adult' child, advocacy for children, the child as gift, and learning as liberation, were all examined in this report. Questions were revisited about the nature of children, of childhood and the church, and answers were sought in the context of a changing world. But complete answers could not be found. There was still much business to be completed, hence the title of this report, *Unfinished Business*. The report was the work of an interdenominational working party, which identified the existence of a common agenda of unfinished business in relation to reaching children on the fringe. We may still ask ourselves the question, 'What unfinished business is there in our churches today?'

The third report, *The Tide is Running Out* (Christian Research, 2000), records the result of the English Church Attendance Survey carried out in 1998 by Dr Peter Brierley of Christian Research. 38,000 local churches received a detailed questionnaire, the results of which were then compared with the 1979 and 1989 English Church Census. The report dramatically spelt out some of the changes that have taken place, especially in relation to children's work. It claimed that one thousand children were leaving the church per week and only two in four churches had children's work on Sundays. The report noted, too, that youth services in the 1990s had kept more teenagers in church than in the 1980s. Questions were asked about what action should be taken to increase the attendance of children. It was noted that some people wanted to come to church but not on Sundays. What method of outreach was needed here? Further, as the patterns of attendance varied between the generations, what did this say about the need for future planning to address different age groups and life stages?

Children may not come regularly to church on Sundays, but most children will respond to genuine love, are open to God and can grasp the concept of Jesus as a friend who cares for them. In the light of these three reports, shifts in priorities are necessary to build a strategy to reach the 87 per cent of children who are untouched by the life of Jesus Christ.

The following strategic action plan may be helpful in identifying the key issues.

Strategy for evangelism

Key point 1: What do we mean by evangelism?

The word 'evangelism' comes from the Greek *euangelizesthai*, meaning 'to announce good news'. The word *euangelion* occurs 72 times in the New Testament, mostly in the writings of Paul.

Read Acts 17:32–34 and 2 Corinthians 4:3–4 and note how these passages show the different ways people respond to the good news. Some respond with repentance and faith, while others are indifferent. Still others reject the good news altogether. One definition of evangelism is to share or announce the good news, but no one particular method is the whole answer. We can use the model of Jesus to see how his approach to people defines what it means to share the good news:
- He listened (for example, to the Samaritan woman at the well in John 4).
- He challenged (as in the case of the rich young ruler in Mark 10:17–23).
- He had time for the outcasts of society (as in the case of the call of Levi in Mark 2:13–17).
- He believed in truth and justice (as in the case of the woman caught in adultery in John 8).

REFLECTION

Read through Luke's Gospel and list how Jesus met the needs of those he came across, while teaching them about God. How does this illustrate the proclamation of the good news? How might this inform outreach to the children on the fringe in your area?

We shouldn't judge evangelism in terms of instant success, rather seeing it as an ongoing 'kingdom activity' that has an impact far beyond a narrow concern for church recruitment. The method of 'up front' preaching needs to become interactive and based on building friendships. Today, relationships are the key to offering the good news beyond the church. We also need to have a better understanding of what goes on in the mind of a child and how children relate to God if we are to identify an appropriate model of evangelism to which they can respond.

Key point 2: Know how children find faith

Many children's leaders have never given any real consideration to the Bible's teaching on the spiritual status of children or have any understanding of what goes on in a child's mind. It is important that we spend time studying the Bible, as this will ultimately affect our ministry with children. As we have already seen, Jesus placed great importance on children and those young in faith, and gives a warning to those who influence their lives (Matthew 18:6). The childhood years are a formative period during which the child is often flexible enough to respond to new stimuli and insights if they are presented in a convincing way. At the same time, attitudes may well be hardening into a settled condition of indifference to God. It is important that children are given the opportunity to respond to God in a way appropriate to their stage of psychological and faith development.

It is at this point that the difficult question of what is meant by conversion needs to be explored. Conversion is a process, no more instantaneous than the process of birth. For this reason it is helpful to talk in terms of people making responses towards Christ, of which they may make many during their lifetime. As the child grows, commitment becomes a natural and necessary form of response. The spiritually developing child experiences a succession of challenges to deepening commitment. It is important to acknowledge children as developing, dependent people. Much of a child's thinking and feeling is dependent on other people—parents, teachers, friends and adults in leadership who shape their world. Children are not merely small adults, and to credit children with adult capacities to think and act is to devalue and even manipulate them.

REFLECTION

Look back at Chapter 8 and remind yourself of the three expressions of faith used by Thomas Groome and quoted by Francis Bridger in *Children Finding Faith*. These are faith as believing, faith as trusting and faith as doing. Now consider the following points:

FAITH AS BELIEVING. How do we help children to build and hold convictions about the essential truths of Christianity? This is an intellectual task requiring content for teaching and learning.

FAITH AS TRUSTING. How do we assist children to build a personal relationship with God, whom they can experience as dependable and trustworthy? This is a relational task, requiring opportunities to experience, reflect, contemplate and enjoy. Prayers, songs, sharing stories, celebrations, worship and family life are all tools for building trust.

FAITH AS DOING. How do we enable children to put into practice the beliefs they are building and a growing relationship with God?

As we consider how children grow in faith, we need to ask why we want to see this happen. This will greatly affect what we are trying to achieve and whether we are directed by God's Spirit as we work with the children. Our aim should be that we want children to have a long-term, loving and developing relationship with God and not simply to represent numbers in the church.

Key point 3: Reaching children through existing programmes

We need to consider what is already happening in the church that could be used as a building block for work with children on the fringe. Is there room to expand? Would the existing children welcome new children? Does what they do fit into the wider life of the church? It might be helpful to visit another church and share these questions with them. This may help us to discover new opportunities and share experiences.

It is important to remember the adults who take care of children at home. The children who come to church bring their home background with them. What programme do our churches have to support parents and carers? Maybe we have a parenting group, an introductory group or a group for new Christians. Being a 'listening ear' when support is needed can be one of the first ways to show concern for people in their day-to-day lives. What long-term strategy exists for reaching the whole church family? Many resources are available to help devise a strategy to reach children on the fringe. The most important thing to remember is to meet the needs of your community and look for opportunities for long-term goals, but with short-term starting dates.

Key point 4: Reaching families in the community

There are many opportunities for reaching out to families in the community, such as playgroups and schools. Different facilities will help us to consider different types of families and to see how this is reflected in the community of the church. The word 'family' can mean different things to different people and it is important to ensure that we use the word in its broadest context. For example, family may mean living with both blood-linked parents, or living with a blood-linked and stepparent. Some children live in homes, are fostered or adopted, or live with only one parent due to divorce or the death of a parent. Our society is constantly changing and unstable, and many people are searching for fixed points. The desire to reach out to families, whatever that may mean, shows that we are being inclusive in our work, just as Christ was inclusive in offering the gospel to all.

As we seek to nurture and befriend those whose lifestyle may be alien to our own, we need to consider the following guidelines:
- Only share with children what you can share with their parents.
- Encourage children to tell their parents what they have done, learned or care about.
- Do not encourage a 'defiant spirit' in the child—a feeling of superiority over his parents because he is, or is becoming, a Christian.
- Keep a steady flow of information going out to the parents.
- Set up family opportunities—outings, parents' evenings and so on.
- Always seek parental support and approval for the activities you are planning.

Key point 5: Reaching wider contacts

Make a list of the different community clubs or organizations involving children and families. Identify members of the congregation who belong to these groups. Consider the opportunities of baptism and ensure that the baptism resources you use are helpful for people who know little about the Christian faith. Look at ways in which the children's ministry team could be involved in the role of preparing families for the baptism of a child. Work with uniformed organizations and develop closer links with uniformed groups in your area.

Key point 6: Not only on a Sunday

Sunday need not be the only day to reach out to children. Midweek clubs are a golden opportunity to reach children in the community. Sunday is no longer a day of rest, but more likely to be a day of relentless activity as people take advantage of the relaxation of shopping regulations. In the past five years there has been a significant growth in midweek clubs which focus on outreach, nurture and community life. Other opportunities include cell groups, which are designed to draw children in and encourage children to minister to each another, and after-school groups.

Consider the following case study. When their M&Ms ran out, a group of Surrey children didn't stampede to the sweet shop. They went to church instead. In their case, M&Ms wasn't the name of their favourite snack, but their favourite midweek club, 'Music and Making', run by their local Anglican church. 'Quite often we used to do stupid songs,' said the club leader Kathryn Copsey. 'It was a fun time. Half the time was singing and making music together—the other half was in making something specific.' Kathryn's own interests were in craft work and music, so the formula worked well. But sadly, the club came to an end three years ago. 'We had to close it down because of lack of personnel,' she said. 'That was a big loss to many of the children there. But the good thing is that many of them have continued a link with the church. It was a way in for them.'

Church buildings aren't usually considered a child-friendly attraction. 'There's something about the courage that it takes to actually go inside a church,' said Kathryn, 'but our club took that "aura" away from the building.'

Since that time, Kathryn has been heading up CURBS (Children in Urban Situations), focusing on youngsters in inner cities and outer urban estates. She finds that midweek clubs work well in that environment. 'Often you get children who are latchkey kids, so what are they going to do after school? A midweek club can serve an important social need in the area.'

Kathryn is a great believer in this type of children's work, and encourages churches to explore running various groups with different themes geared to reaching both active, sporty children and those who prefer quiet crafts or music. 'Churches have an incredible opportunity to respond to the government's call for after-school clubs,' she says, 'by providing space for kids to come—and just to be there to support them in their homework.' The government is encouraging the idea of clubs to help meet the needs of youngsters who are potentially at risk after school. Churches can help urban children who don't have space at home to get on with their studies—and those who may otherwise be playing out on the streets.

Another example of this type of outreach is Kidz Clubs. In the spring of 1994 the Frontline Community Church in Liverpool started a weekly club on Saturday mornings, adopting Bill Wilson's model of Metro Ministries in Brooklyn, New York, which included weekly home visits to every child. Starting with 40 children a week, there are now as many as

700 children attending the club. The key factor is the close personal relationships built up, which help children to feel that they are special individuals.

Key point 7: Reaching children through church celebrations

Special celebrations give churches an opportunity to reach out into the community. Below are pointers for action:
- Be simple: tell the story of celebration.
- Start where people are in their lives. For instance, use the opportunity of Mothering Sunday or St Valentine's Day to affirm motherhood and marriage.
- Integrate celebrations with activities to give Christian teaching over the course of the year.
- Celebrations need to be for all ages: include something for everyone.
- Celebrations are a wonderful opportunity for using pictures, puppets, visual aids, such as a crib, action and so on.
- Celebrations can help to reclaim a Christian perspective, for example, putting Christ at the centre of Christmas, demonstrating that Good Friday is a holy day, Pentecost as a major Christian festival and so on.
- Schools represent a major opportunity for the church to provide resources (people and ideas) to mark and celebrate key festivals.
- Creative publicity, such as invitations, posters and so on, are an important means of outreach into the community.
- Create competitions at Christmas, Easter and Pentecost. Use celebrations for fund-raising ideas and themes for fairs. Distribute publicity well in advance through local schools. Choose artwork that helps tell the story. Names of competition winners and runners up can be announced at the fair and displayed afterwards in local shops, the foyer of the local bank and so on.

Key point 8: Reaching the local school

Consider how a positive partnership between church and school can be set up. Ask the following questions:
- Is it a positive or negative experience when church and school come together?

- Does the church know, or how can the church know, what is happening in school?
- Does the school know, or how can the school know, what is happening in church?

Consider the potential of contributing in the following ways:

Within the school community
- Serving as foundation governors.
- Contributing to the school worship programmes on a regular basis.
- Helping with RE provision through teaching and supporting staff.
- Offering pastoral assistance for the school community through regular contact.

Within the church community
- Offering the church as a resource, such as a place of worship for special celebrations (Harvest, Christmas, leavers' service and so on).
- Offering the church building and its history as a curriculum resource.
- Offering nurture through children's clubs, playgroups, special events, holiday clubs, sponsored activities, parade services for uniformed organizations and so on.

Further action

Decide what is the most effective approach to the task of reaching out to children on the fringe in your particular situation. What action will you take to put into practice this new thinking? How would you sell your ideas to your church leaders?

Selected bibliography

All God's Children? Report (1991)
Unfinished Business Report (1995)
The Tide is Running Out (Christian Research, 2000)

Appendix 1

SETTING UP A MIDWEEK CLUB

The following sample was prepared originally by a former student at London Bible College, Becky Holland, as a result of a practical placement, and is reproduced here with her permission. The material could be used with slight adaptations in a variety of settings, including during the school day, after school or at weekends, depending on need.

The objectives of this sample are:
- To indicate the main issues in setting up a children's club.
- To explore how to adapt the issues to a particular situation.
- To create tailored exercises to help explore those issues.
- To examine resources available to help set up a club.
- To provide information to start a club from scratch.

In order to help identify some of the main issues in setting up a children's club, take a sheet of A4 paper and write 'Setting up a children's club' in the middle. Put a circle round this heading and then attach bubbles around it, containing any issues that come to mind. If any other related issues come to mind, attach them to the appropriate bubble. You may wish to add to this 'mind map' at a later stage.

Main issues might include:
- Aims
- Staffing
- Health and safety
- Programme and resources
- Support from the church

Aims

It is possible to run a children's club without having thought through why we are doing it in the first place, except that it seems like a good idea. We may find that members of the team have aims in mind which are unspoken or half thought through. However, when the aims are clear, they can be brought to bear upon many decisions in setting up and running the club. Clear aims will affect the materials needed, the programme and how the children are approached.

Write in no more than fifty words a Mission Statement for the club. Compare your statement with the aims below.

- To challenge children to accept Jesus Christ as their friend and Saviour and to nurture them in their growing relationship with him.
- To encourage children and their families to become part of God's family within their local church.
- To help children to attain a wholeness of life by sharing in spiritual, physical, social and intellectual experiences.
- To provide an opportunity for children to serve within the church and the community.
- To provide a means of outreach to all children.

Your aims may be short-term goals rather than the long-term goals listed above. The type of children for whom the club is catering will dictate the objectives to a certain extent, and will have to be clearly defined from the start. Is the club to cater for children in the church, outside the church or both? This will affect the materials you use and the way you use Bible material—or even the use of the Bible at all to begin with, as children outside the church will have little or no familiarity with it.

Age range

If the age range is too wide (for example, 4–14), how will you cater for all tastes and abilities? Large age ranges may attract many children to the club quickly. This raises questions about staffing and health and safety regulations.

Will your group have a narrow age range—for example, 7–9? Will you limit the group to members from one school only, if it is an after-school club? Or will children be able to bring similar aged friends from other schools?

Venue

The most obvious venue might be the church hall or a similar building if it is appropriate for frequent use by children. How much space is at your disposal? Is the space sufficient for the number of children you anticipate coming? Do you intend to play games, which require a lot of space to be safe?

Is there a reliable heating supply for the cold winter months? Are there sufficient toilet facilities for both sexes? Are there kitchen facilities for making light refreshments?

Almost as important is the 'feeling' of the hall. It is child-friendly? The atmosphere in the hall should be bright, light and colourful if possible. It is important that the children have somewhere to sit. If this is the floor, it must not be dirty or cold, having at least a carpeted area on which to fit all the children.

How much furniture is at your disposal? Are there enough tables suitable for craft work, or will the church invest in some good-quality foldaway tables for your use? Are there facilities to use a television and video if necessary? Are there any storage facilities for the resources you will need to buy (and accumulate)?

When the club is established, you will need to think about preservation of both the children and the hall. Are there any areas of the hall that will be out-of-bounds for the children and need cordoning off? The children will definitely not be allowed unsupervised in the kitchen area, but what about the back of a church stage, other raised area or the tempting pile of stacked chairs? Or perhaps there may be precious furniture such as the church altar or chairs, which will need protection from sticky fingers or clambering primary-aged children.

There is important legislation regarding some of the matters mentioned above. This is covered in the section on Health and Safety on pages 199–200.

Imagine yourself in the venue you have chosen. Is it suitable for the club? Go through the questions above and write a checklist. Tick off the questions you can answer positively. Underline the questions you can't answer. Keep the list for future reference.

Timing and frequency

Check when other clubs or activities are running in your area and avoid clashing with them. Which night do the Brownies, Cubs or majorettes club meet? Will the end of football practice coincide with the first half-hour of the club? Does the school chess club play in the same lunch hour as your proposed club?

Consider how long you intend the club to run each week or fortnight. The Children's Act 1989 requires a club to be registered with the local authorities if it runs activities for the under-8s and lasts for two hours or more, and takes place on more than six days per year. Many clubs run comfortably for around an hour and a half (excluding setting-up and packing-away time), but it is advisable to read the relevant parts of the Act and put into practice anything that would benefit the children.

Staffing

There are also guidelines in *The Children Act* regarding adult-to-child ratios. Children under 7 years old need two adults for up to eight children. For children over 7 years old, there should also be two adults for up to eight children, but an additional two adults for every additional twelve children are needed. If, therefore, your club has 28 children, eight of whom are under 7 years old and twenty over 7, you will need two leaders for the first eight children, two leaders for the second eight children and two extra for the remaining twelve children. This makes a total of six leaders. This must be the absolute minimum for the number of children involved. It is a good thing to have a few extra 'floating' volunteers who can step in when needed. For other more unusual activities, such as outdoor pursuits and swimming, staff numbers need checking before you set off.

If you are running a school lunch club, there may be Christian teachers who will be happy to give you a hand. If the club is church-based, there may be others in the congregation who will help you. You may even be able to enlist the help of another church's youth worker or other volunteers. When approaching other churches, it is a good idea to tread gently, in case it is perceived that you are stealing their volunteers!

Many churches enlist the help of totally unsuitable members of their congregation. This is partly for lack of understanding about the task in hand. Some people are encouraged to work with children as leaders because it's seen as a 'safe' ministry. This attitude is not helpful for the person involved and could be damaging to the children. Secondly, churches are desperate for someone to take on the children's club, and will use anyone who is willing. There are always very kind people in the congregation who will volunteer for anything, even if it is not their gift. This too can be damaging. It is better to wait until the right leaders come along than to ill-equip a children's project with unsuitable leaders.

The help of willing teenagers can also be enlisted, providing they are gifted with children. It is good sometimes to take sensible risks, and thereby encourage and use the talents of younger people. However, it has to be said that the teenagers must be in addition to the required number of adult leaders per child.

Adult leaders should:
- be open to God's call to ministry
- be strong in their Christian faith
- have empathy with children, like and be liked by children, and relate well to parents
- display leadership qualities and communicate well
- be team workers
- be able to listen, to be consistent, stable and patient, and to show commitment
- be able to discipline sensitively
- be willing to be trained and to train others, and relate to church councils

The above qualities are unlikely to be found in one person, let alone be exhibited in every member of your team. Some of the qualities may lie dormant until the leader is faced with a particular challenge. Esther Bailey writes that we are all 'visual aids' for God and, instead of feeling daunted, we should recognize that we have an important part to play in our work as children's leaders (*Running Christian Groups in Schools*, Scripture Union, 1998). Amazing gifts can develop in each of us when we step out in faith and service.

Legislation

The Children Act of 1989 strongly recommends that all children's leaders sign a form giving their personal details, name, address, telephone number and assurance that they have never been convicted of an offence, sexual or otherwise, against children or young people. Other details about hobbies, interests or relevant qualifications would also be helpful. All children's workers should fill in this form. Explain that it is vital for the safety and protection of everyone concerned.

As a short exercise, design an A4 form, taking all these issues into account. Make sure you include a space for the person to sign and write the date. You could include spaces for referees.

Training

Training for yourself and your staff members need not be tedious. Apart from the many helpful books now available on children's ministry, there are a variety of exciting courses (some quite reasonably priced) that you can attend. These can be single days (usually Saturdays), whole weekends, or midweek. You can often obtain details from magazines aimed at Christian children's workers, or by putting yourself on the mailing lists of organizations such as BRF, Scripture Union and CPAS. If you are studying through a distance learning children's ministry course, why not suggest that some of your colleagues also try it out?

Health and safety

Health and safety is a crucial part of running a children's club. We have already considered the importance of having the right number of staff and the suitability of the venue. There will inevitably be a certain number of scraped knees and bumped elbows to deal with over the course of a club session. Games are wonderful for letting off steam and pent-up energy after a day in the classroom (especially if it has been raining and the children have had no outside play), but you will need to ensure that younger children are not in danger of being hurt by their older companions. It is advisable to have a strict lower age limit in order to preserve the smaller ones and still let the older children have fun.

It is also vital that you have a well-stocked and regularly checked first-aid kit on the premises. Reasonably priced ones are available from most chemists. There may be occasions when a more serious accident takes place and it is important that there is at least one leader in your team who carries a valid First Aid Certificate. Certificates can be obtained through the Red Cross or St John Ambulance, who run courses, usually over three days or a series of evenings. The details are easy to find in your local library, community or family centre, or through the local council. Courses can be quite expensive, and leaders may need to be sponsored by the church to enable them to attend.

All accidents must be recorded in a special book and the child's parent informed immediately.

Registering the children

It is important to have all the relevant details about each child so that a parent can be contacted in emergencies. A returnable form must be sent out to all parents/carers with:
- permission for the child(ren) to attend the club
- the child(ren)'s name(s)
- address of the parent
- emergency contact telephone number(s)
- the age of the child
- any illnesses or allergies the child may have

For the child's own safety, it is important to have these details *before* the child attends the club. (A sample form is shown on the next page.) Each child's attendance must be registered every week.

Parental Consent Form

I give my permission for [child's name] _____

to be involved in the activities organized by the

[name of club] _____ club of

[name of church] _____ Church, which take

place between [start time] _____ and [finish time] _____

on a [day] _____ during term time.

I understand that all the activities will be properly supervised by adults. I give my permission for the leaders to act on my behalf as a parent if I cannot be contacted in an emergency.

BLOCK CAPITALS PLEASE

Parent/carer's name _____

Address _____

_____

_____

Child's date of birth _____

Medical conditions that we should be aware of, e.g. Asthma/allergies

_____

_____

_____

Signature of Parent/Carer _____

Telephone Number _____

Other contact _____

Telephone Number _____

Discipline

There may be certain children in your club who are continually disruptive or aggressive. This is often hard for the leaders to deal with and unpleasant for the other children concerned. While understanding that such disruptive children may have reasons for their behaviour, it is also important that the other children are safe and enjoy the club atmosphere.

It is important to establish some club ground rules from the very first meeting, and for the children at all times to be aware of the standards of behaviour required and the things that will not be tolerated. It is very easy for some children to take over a club and make it a miserable place for the others to be.

Ground rules should be printed, read out and displayed for the children to see. If possible, a copy, including disciplinary procedures, should be sent home for the parents/carers to see, so that they encourage the children to abide by the club rules. Stress that these rules are for the benefit of all the children and that they are in place for the safety and fun of all concerned. Of course, no child should *ever* be physically punished in any way whatsoever.

Write down a list of behaviours or actions that you would consider unacceptable for children in your club (for example, fighting, swearing, and so on). Separate these into two groups—that behaviour which is dangerous, and that which is not so serious but will be disruptive if repeated. In this way you can devise a two-tier system for discipline.

One particular club runs a red and yellow card system, similar to that in football. For less serious behaviour, a yellow card is 'presented' to the child as a warning (for example, if a child is very rude or continually disruptive). This card is recorded in a special book. If the child continues to misbehave, another yellow card is given, and this 'translates' into a red card. The red card means that the child is banned from the club for *one week only*. Of course a red card can be given immediately if the child seriously assaults another child or causes serious danger to another child. It should also be noted that, for extreme bad behaviour, the child can be immediately taken home by *two* adult leaders. Parents should be informed sensitively if their child has received a card, at the discretion of the club's leaders.

Children should be banned completely from the club only in consultation with the parents and the child, and only in the most serious of circumstances.

Positive disciplining

The red and yellow card form of discipline can produce a fairly effective method of 'crowd-control' and can often prevent bad behaviour from escalating into something worse.

However, bad behaviour can be a helpful sign that something is not quite right—for example, a programme with not enough physical activity, or an uninspiring or slow-moving programme, which children tire of very easily. We should first look to our programme to see if it is not stimulating the children enough and thereby causing boredom to turn into disruption.

If this is not the case (and you will only find this out by asking the children), it may be that the children who misbehave have other problems. I am not suggesting that you ask them what their problems are—children's leaders should never act as amateur psychologists—but a disruptive child may need more one-to-one supervision and care.

Children often behave badly to gain attention. Of course, arbitrary attention will not help the child. Constant acceptance, whatever the child has done, affirmation and building up the child's self-esteem over time can be very effective. As a rule of thumb, children always seem to behave better when we expect more of them.

One way to build up a child's self-esteem and help them to be less disruptive is to keep a record card that is only to be seen by the child concerned and the supervising adult. The card would be used weekly for recording the achievements of the child, and could work towards some kind of privilege, such as stickers, sweets or 'golden time' when the child chooses a favourite game or activity. Keep the tasks simple, for example, 'I will try hard not to shout in club today' or 'I will try hard not to fight my sister at club today'. Children are generally pleased with their achievements and may gradually learn to control themselves without being asked. It will be their achievements, rather than the rewards, which will eventually build the children's self-esteem.

Another way of helping a child learn to control his or her anger is to have a quiet corner, furnished maybe with beanbag seats, books, colouring pens and paper. The children should know that this is a safe place to go, just to sit and cool off, be quiet and read or colour, or maybe just a safe place away from other children. The quiet corner is not for punishment where children are sent, but a place of their own just to be. With positive discipline and genuine care and sensitivity, some children's disruptive behaviour turns dramatically to trust, co-operation and real enjoyment at the club.

Programme and resources

People are more important than programmes. A club where the programme is slick and fast-moving with up-to-date resources, but where the leaders still do not know the names of the children, is not a good model. Whatever programme is chosen or designed for the club, the most important element is the children.

The programme has to be designed with our own particular group in mind. Their culture, songs, TV programmes, heroes and fads are all very important to them, and we need to relate to the children on their own territory. We should familiarize ourselves with those little details, the children's likes and dislikes, the football team they support, their favourite pop star (at the moment), where they go on holiday and whether their grandmother has a dog or a budgie! It is important to each child that the leaders know his or her name.

Relating to culture

The world today is very visual and children are used to having their attention grabbed with videos, films and computer games, so the programme needs to be fairly fast-moving, with a lot of activity, variety and visual aids. Generally speaking, though, children still love to hear stories, and any that relate to them or capture their imagination will be received well.

Using the Bible with children

Using the Bible with children needs care and attention. A good-quality children's Bible should be used and passages that relate to the child's experience selected. Complicated theological passages should be avoided and children should never be left at the end of the club session with disturbing questions that their own parents or carers can't answer. Bear in mind the original context of the story and do not bend the story or stretch its meaning to fit your teaching theme. Avoid passages that raise awkward questions, such as David's adultery and the more brutal war passages of the Old Testament. Many children who attend the club will have little or no Bible awareness and this is not the time to plunge into the deep end. A better idea is to start off with a story like the creation account in Genesis, which is a gloriously colourful way to begin, with vast amounts of resources on the subject. All children can relate to the world around them, and will be fascinated to look at aspects of it further.

Activities

As you get to know the children in your club, so you will be able to strike a balanced programme and know the kind of things they respond well to. All children love to play, but not all children love rough-and-tumble chasing games. Ask the children their opinion. They will soon tell you if something is boring! What activities do they like? Most children love making things and painting. Not all children find it easy to read the words on puzzle sheets and wordsearches. Some may need less wordy art activities.

Consider the following activities:

Games

Relays, tag, Giants and Dwarves, Swim Fishy Swim, sitting down games such as Chinese Whispers, Duck Duck Goose, acting games such as Captain's Aboard, mime, collecting games such as Chinese Laundry and so on. The children will often suggest the favourite games that they play at school.

Crafts

Painting, designing, model building (individual, group and giant), papier mâché, festive card design (for example, Mother's Day, Christmas, Valentine's Day), animal masks, puppets, bookmarks, banners, musical instruments such as rain sticks, paper flowers, baskets, salt-dough animals, Fimo models, simple cooking, such as biscuits or sugar mice—the list is endless.

Activities that engage

Singing, Bible stories, secular modern and traditional stories such as the *Chronicles of Narnia* by C.S. Lewis, Christian videos suitable for children (serialized perhaps at 15 to 20 minutes per session), puzzles, quizzes, poetry, prayer, memory verses, colouring sheets, short talks (five minutes maximum), discussion (in small groups)—this list, too, is endless.

Putting the programme together

There are many good resources on the market with ideas and suggestions for a children's club programme. These can be used and adapted as required. Adapting ideas might seem daunting at first, but it gets easier with practice. You will soon be able to gauge roughly how long you need for different activities and you'll then be able to divide the allotted time into bite-sized chunks. Set up the hall ready for the children's arrival so that you can give them your full attention. Have all your equipment laid out. If the club runs for an hour and a half, the session may look something like this:

6.00 pm

Children arrive and register. Organize a game they can join without explanation.

6.05 pm

Energetic warm-up game such as Captain's Aboard, to burn off a bit of energy. This game might link into a theme, for example, Noah or Jonah.

6.15 pm
Quieter second game such as Duck Duck Goose, or a similar sitting circle tag game to quieten the children down.

6.30 pm
Crafts in small groups.

6.50 pm
Refreshments such as squash and biscuits, served during the last ten minutes of the craft session.

7.00 pm
Clearing away craft activity and tidying the hall. Encourage the children to help with this.

7.10 pm
Choice time in which the children can choose either a relevant Bible story, video episode, talk or game, all of which are running simultaneously. Children respond well to this and the smaller group tends to foster a quieter atmosphere for those wanting to really listen and participate in discussion.

7.25 pm
Prayer.

7.30 pm
Home time.

Small groups

Children tend to work better in established small groups. You could allot one or more of the same leaders each week to assist the same group, to provide continuity and build up relationships. When new children join, they can immediately be put into a group with at least one good friend. The groups could be given names, for example Bears, Dolphins, Tigers and Giraffes, and each child could make a badge with their group symbol on it. This system is also good for splitting children up sensitively into teams for games without the embarrassment of 'not being wanted' by a particular team or the chaos of asking the children to get themselves into small groups.

Resources

Running Christian Groups in Schools, E. Bailey (Scripture Union, 1998)
This is a good, comprehensive book which is useful not just in schools but also for after-school clubs. It contains helpful suggestions about discipline in children's clubs and has an excellent resources section.

Going Bananas, S. Clutterham (Scripture Union, 1997)
Fast-moving and impressive holiday club material; needs a big team and a bit of experience. One of many SU holiday club resources on offer.

Leading a Kid's Club in Your Church, V. Cracknell (Joint Board of Christian Education, Australia)
A comprehensive book on children's clubs with nothing overlooked except British legislation on *The Children Act*. Even then, the author's suggestions seem to take the main issues into account. Includes a comprehensive theology of ministry to children, training, assessment and evaluation. May need adapting slightly to British culture.

Building New Bridges, C. Gibb (NS/CHP, 1996)
Material designed especially for after-school clubs giving comprehensive and clear instructions about setting up. Well balanced for fun and activity. Good section on *The Children Act* 1989.

All of the above publications provide reference about other resources, such as books on crafts and games, that you might find helpful.

Bibles

The Lion Storyteller Bible, B. Hartman (Lion Publishing, 1995)
This is a book of selected Bible stories rewritten specially for reading aloud. The stories are compact, easy to understand, beautifully illustrated and very suitable for the under-8s. The death and resurrection of Jesus are presented sensitively and movingly.

The Lion Children's Bible, P. Alexander (Lion Publishing, 1992)
This is the whole Bible in two volumes reproduced with children in mind. It is clear and concise, with language suitable for children up to 11 or 12 years old.

The International Children's Bible, New Century Version (Word)
This Bible is written in language suitable for 6- to 12-year-olds. It is especially good for memory verses as the language is so clear. The hardback version has beautiful illustrations.

The Good News Bible, Second Edition (Bible Society/HarperCollins, 1994)
An excellent translation for use with children, with illustrations that are fun to trace or reproduce for easy visual aids.

The Contemporary English Version of the Bible (*Into the Light*) (Bible Society/HarperCollins, 1997)
A fresh, readable translation of the Bible from the original languages.

Organizations for resources and training.
Church Pastoral Aid Society, Athena Drive, Tachbrook Park, Warwick, CV34 6NG. Telephone: 01926 33422

Crusaders, 2 Romeland Hill, St Albans, Herts, AL3 4ET. Telephone: 01727 855422

Scripture Union, 207 Queensway, Bletchley, Milton Keynes, MK2 2EB. Telephone: 01908 856000 (also Schools Ministry Network and Scripture Union in Schools)

National Christian Education Council, 1020 Bristol Road, Selly Oak, Birmingham, B29 6LB. Telephone: 0121 472242

Prayer and evaluation

The busyness of a club often means that praying together as a team gets pushed into the background or squeezed into the five minutes before the club starts. It is helpful to get together and pray for the children's work as regularly as possible. The bigger the group of volunteers, the harder it seems to co-ordinate a time to get together. One way to overcome this is to split into two groups at different times with a small prayer agenda, and then make sure both groups get feedback. Children's work is often hard and demanding. Support and unity in the team are invaluable and praying together cements that unity.

Evaluating the work is vital for its growth and development. Try to have regular team meetings to discuss how things are going. This can be the same time as the prayer, which may naturally grow out of evaluation. Keep a simple record of how each session went, noting any activities that did not work and briefly saying why. Note, too, the things that went well or could have done with a little adaptation. Note suggestions from team members and be willing to try them out. Often, a simple adjustment can transform the way things happen: for example, instead of shouting yourself hoarse when explaining a craft activity to a 30-strong bunch of lively kids, simply duplicate the instructions and hand a copy to each group leader to use quietly.

Draft a simple evaluation form covering the relevant elements for feedback. This need take no more than five minutes to complete each week.

Church support

Maintaining regular links with your church and its leadership team is vitally important. Every book on children's ministry is concerned that the work can be very lonely, especially if people think we are doing a very good job and they can just leave us to it. The children's team needs encouragement and mentoring in order to grow and learn. Ensure that regular meetings are arranged with someone in authority in the church (and/or school) and that your own life does not get overlooked.

It is also important to maintain regular contact with the congregation to let them know how the children's club is going. Think of three ways, taking about five minutes each, of keeping the congregation informed. Then think of ways in which the congregation could help the club. People make excellent resources, too. What gifts are represented in your congregation that could benefit the children's club?

Finance

Financially, the club need not be too demanding upon the church. However, a church's budget is usually a good yardstick by which to measure its priorities. The church may lend your club the use of the OHP, but can it stretch to a set of good-quality children's Bibles or even a parachute for parachute games? The chances are that if your church has employed a full-time paid youth worker, there will be a budget, however small, for equipment to run the club. If the church cannot afford to employ youth staff, you may consider making a small charge to the children of, say, 20–25p per child per week. This usually covers the juice and biscuits during the club and over a period of time may amount to sufficient money to purchase a few extra resources.

Networking

Often it will help to pool resources, ideas and support with other churches and children's workers. Well-established groups may be able to offer advice and encouragement. It is great to meet and get to know other people who are in the same situation, and sharing ideas and experiences can often lift the burden of worry that newcomers in particular might be feeling.

There are also support groups available to help. Contact your diocesan office if you attend an Anglican church, or your local Baptist youth officer. The Network of Christian Schools' Workers has regular conferences to meet, share ideas and encourage one another.

Publicity

If your club takes place on school premises, you may get permission to put up posters or have fliers handed out in classes. A great way to reach all the children at once is to take part in a school assembly, where the club can be presented in an interesting and exciting way. Schools are not the place for overt evangelism and any work undertaken in schools should be done sensitively.

If the children's club is an after-school event, again, approaching a few local schools would be helpful, or advertising in the local press, with all the details of the club and perhaps a little about the church. If budget, time and staffing allow, running a small holiday club during the school holidays might attract new children into the club. There are many holiday club books on the market which include fairly comprehensive instructions for beginners.

There may also be outlets in the church that might publicize the club, such as the parent and toddlers group. Some parents may have older children who would like to come to the club. Publicize your club well in advance in the church news letter.

Once the club is established, it might be helpful to put together a package or small booklet about the club. This could be used to give to church members to help them to pray, to parents considering the club for their children, as an introduction for schools, or as a tool for fundraising. Why not get the children to help with the task? They could draw pictures or even write a few sentences about the club for inclusion in the booklet.

Reading list

The Adventure Begins: a practical guide to exploring the Bible with the under-12s, T. Clutterham (Scripture Union and CPAS, 1996)

Children Finding Faith, F. Bridger (Scripture Union, 1988)

All God's Children (National Society and Church House Publishing, 1991)

The Schools Work Handbook, Emlyn Williams (Scripture Union, 1996)

Appendix 2

EVALUATION FORM

This evaluation form can be used as a generic guide for any children's ministry work.

General assessment

1. What is my aim? _____

2. What are my short-term objectives? _____

3. What evidence do I have that my understanding of the group is increasing? _____

4. What are the signs that I am achieving my objectives as listed above?

5. What resources are available for me to use? _____

6. To what extent are there problems that still need resolving?

Session assessment

1. What was the aim of the session? _____

2. What evidence is there that this aim came across and was understood by the group? _____

3. Did I use a variety of methods? _____

4. Did I sense that I kept the group with me right through? _____

5. How did I involve the group in worship? _____

6. How did I involve the group in learning? _____

7. What action, if any, should I take as a result of this session?

Appendix 3

COMMISSIONING SERVICE

This commissioning service is suitable for use with all those working with children and young people in the church.

Minister: *(To team leaders)* God has called you to nurture our children and young people in the Christian faith and to help them grow to maturity in Christ. We shall ask you to promise before God and this church family that you accept the responsibility of this ministry on behalf of your church.

(To congregation) It is our responsibility as a congregation to pray that God by his Holy Spirit will equip our children and youth team with wisdom, love and the care and patience they will need. So let us thank God for their willingness to serve him among the children and young people of our church.

As we worship God together, let us rededicate ourselves, as the children and youth team, and as a congregation, to serve Christ.

(To leaders) As followers of Jesus Christ, and members of his Church, will you promise to be consistent in your own personal life and witness?

Team leaders: Yes, by God's grace and guidance, we will.

Minister: Will you be faithful to the Gospel of Jesus Christ and conscientious in your ministry?

Team leaders: Yes, with the help of the Lord, we will.

Minister: Will you love and care for the individuals in your group, and pray regularly for them?

Team leaders: Yes, with the help of God, we will.

Minister: Will you pray and worship with the congregation of this Church as often as you can?

Team leaders: By the Spirit of God, we will.

Minister: As team leaders we say a prayer of personal commitment together.

Team leaders: Lord Jesus, I believe you have called me into ministry among the children and young people in this church community. Help me to remember the importance of the work you have given me to do. Give me your love for the children and young people in my care. Keep me faithful to the promises I have just made and to ask for all the strength and wisdom I need from you. Amen.

Minister: May God bless you, and show you his love daily through the power of his Spirit. In the name of Jesus Christ, our Lord and Saviour.

Minister: (*To the congregation*) As the task of reaching and teaching children (and young people) is the task of the whole Church, will you remember these groups—members, leaders and helpers—regularly in your prayers?

Congregation: By the grace of God, we will.

Minister: Will you take full interest in this ministry, supporting the children and youth teams wherever you can, introducing new members, and welcoming children and young people into the life of the Church?

Congregation: With the help of God, we will.

Minister: Let us remember our partnership in sharing the gospel of good news with our children and young people.
(*Children and young people could be invited to come to the front of church to pray for leaders alongside congregation.*)

All: We thank you, heavenly Father, for our children and young people; for their enthusiasm and energy, for their openness, curiosity and trustfulness. May the family life of this church show them that they belong as members with us, in the body of Christ. Help us to be faithful in praying for them, that they may be strengthened in their faith and equipped to live in today's world. Amen.

Appendix 4

Towards a Charter for Children in the Church

1. Children are equal partners in the life of the church.
2. The full diet of Christian worship is for children as well as adults.
3. Learning is for the whole church, adults and children.
4. Fellowship is for all—each belonging meaningfully to the rest.
5. Service is for children to give, as well as adults.
6. The call to evangelism comes to all God's people, of whatever age.
7. The Holy Spirit speaks powerfully through children as well as adults.
8. The discovery and development of gifts in children and adults is a key function of the church.
9. As a church community we must learn to do in separate age groups only those things which in all conscience we cannot do together.
10. The concept of the Priesthood of all Believers includes children.

Source: United Reform Church

Using the charter

If your church adopts this charter, the congregation may need to think through the implications of changes in attitude and practice that might be necessary. Below are some questions to assist this process.

1. How do you perceive children?
   - As plants that unfold from within as they are nurtured?
   - As raw material to be shaped from without through teaching and discipline?

In what ways are adult perceptions of children affecting how children are treated in the church?

2. What are the prevailing beliefs about children in relation to God in your church? In what ways do they help or hinder children in feeling that they are welcome and that they belong?
3. Consider the locality in which your church is placed. What provision is already made to support parents in their parenting—for example, drop-in centres, playgroups, health centres, access areas? Are there any ways in which your church might better serve the locality by working alongside others or initiating new ventures that will help to enhance the home life of children?
4. The church may need to take both a prophetic and pastoral role in its work with and for children. In what ways is this already happening and in what ways is it not? What might need to change?
5. Imagine you are a child in your locality. What would help you to feel wanted and accepted there? Is there anything missing, for example, safe places to play and meet friends, clubs? In what ways might Christians need to be advocates for children in your locality?

Bibliography

Introduction

A Little Child Shall Lead Them, Arnold, Plough Publishing, 1997
Children at Risk, Porter, Kingsway, 1998
Realities of Childhood, Inchley, SU, 1987
Letters to Children, Lewis, Collins Fount Paperbacks, 1985
Learn to Discern, Moss, Zondervan Publishing House, 1992
Amusing Ourselves to Death, Postman, Methuen, 1995
Whose Child? Wilson, Creation House, 1992

Children and God

Children of the King, Buckland, Anzea, 1979
Children and God, Buckland, SU, 1988
Tuesday's Child, Christian Education Publication, 2001
All About Children, Inchley, Coverdale, 1976
Children of Abraham, Kingdon, Carey, 1973
Early Harvest, Prince, Falcon, 1976
Whose is the Kingdom? Prince, Scripture Union, 1979

Biblical perspectives

Special Children? Lane, Grace Publications, 1996
Children's Ministry, Richards, Zondervan, 1983
Children in the Early Church, Strange, Paternoster, 1996
Jesus and the Children, Weber, Geneva WCC, 1979
The Church and Childhood, Wood (ed.), Blackwell, 1994
Anthropology of the Old Testament, Wolff, SCM Press, 1974
God's People in God's Land, Wright, Eerdmans/Paternoster, 1990
Precious in His Sight, Zuck, Baker Books, 1996

Whatever happened to childhood?

Centuries of Childhood, Aries, Penguin, 1986
Kindness to Strangers, Boswell, Peregrine, 1989
The Politics of Childhood, Hoyle, Journeyman, 1989
The History of Childhood, Lloyd de Mause (ed.), Aronson, 1991
Childhood in the Middle Ages, Shahar, Routledge, 1991

The child's social world

Children and Prejudice, Aboud, Blackwell, 1998
Taking Care, Armstrong, NCB, 1991
Child Poverty and Deprivation in UK, Bradshaw, NCB, 1990
Street Children, Butcher, Nelson Word, 1996
Seven Things Children Need, Drescher, Monarch, 1988
Poverty and Inequality in UK: Effects on Children, Kumar, NCB, 1993
Childhood—A Multicultural View, Konner, Little, Brown, 1991
Children and the Environment, Rosenbaum, NCB, 1993
The Child in the City, Ward, Bedford, 1990
The Child in the Country, Ward, Bedford, 1988

Child development

Dibs: In Search of Self, Axline, Penguin, 1990
Child Care and the Growth of Love, Bowlby, Penguin, 1965
Baby & Child from Birth to Age 5, Leach, Penguin, 1988
When Children Suffer, Lester, Westminster Press, Philadelphia, 1987
The Needs of Children, Kellmer Pringle, Routledge, 1992
Grand parenting, Kesler/Parsons, Hodder and Stoughton, 1994
The Sixty Minute Father, Parsons, Hodder and Stoughton, 1995
A Father's Place, Pytches, Hodder and Stoughton, 1993
The Sixty Minute Mother, Parsons, Hodder and Stoughton, 1999
Understanding Children's Development, Smith & Cowie, Blackwell, 1991
Helping Children Cope with Divorce, Wells, Sheldon Press, 1993

How children think

Making Sense, Bruner & Haste (ed.), Routledge, 1993
Christian Child Development, Cully, Gill & MacMillan, 1980
Children's Minds, Donaldson, Fontana, 1987
Religious Thinking from Childhood to Adolescence, Goldman, Routledge & Kegan Paul, 1964
Readiness for Religion, Goldman, Routledge & Kegan Paul, 1965
Religious Thinking & Religious Education—A Critique of Goldman, Howkins, Tyndale Press, 1965
Will my Rabbit Go to Heaven? Hughes, Lion, 1988
The Grasp of Consciousness, Piaget, Routledge, 1977
Counselling Children through the World of Play, Sweeney, Tyndale, 1997

Spirituality and faith development

Christian Perspectives on Faith Development, Astley & Francis, Gracewing, 1992
Caring for the Whole Child, Bradford, The Children's Society, 1995
Children Finding Faith (2nd edition), Bridger, SU/CPAS, 2000
The Religious Potential of the Child, Cavalletti, LTP, 1992
The Spiritual Life of Children, Coles, HarperCollins, 1992
How Faith Grows, General Synod Board of Education, NS/CHP, 1991
Fostering Faith, Francis & Chamberlain, Paulist Press, 1988
Faith Development and Fowler, Dykstra, CREP, 1986
Stages of Faith, Fowler, HarperCollins, 1981
Faith Development & Pastoral Care, Fowler, Fortress Press, 1987
Looking Beyond, Fuller, Kevin Mayhew, 1996
Christian Religious Education, Groome, Harper and Row, 1979
The Spirit of the Child, Hay & Nye, HarperCollins, 1998
Exploring Children's Spiritual Formation, Morgenthaler (ed.), Pillars Press, 1999
The Original Vision, Robinson, Religious Experience Research Unit, 1977
Making Sense of Spiritual Development, Smith, Stapleford Centre, 1999
Don't Just Do Something, Sit There, Stone, RMEP, 1995

Will our Children Have Faith? Westerhoff III, Seabury, 1980
Bringing Up Children in the Christian Faith, Westerhoff III, Winston, 1980

Belonging to the worshipping community

Issues in the Christian Initiation of Children, Brown and Sokal (ed.), LTP, 1989
Children in the Assembly of the Church, Bernstein & Brooks-Leonards (eds.), Liturgy Training Publications, 1992
The Good Shepherd and the Child, Coulter, The Catechist of the Good Shepherd Publications, 1994
His Spirit Is With Us, Francis, Collins, 1981
Making Contact, Francis, Collins, 1986
Seen and Heard, Cray, CPAS, 1995
Children in the Church Today, Sister Magdalene, St Vladimir Seminary Press, 1991
Children in Worship: Lessons from Research, Morgenthaler, Becker & Bertls, Pillars Press, 1999
Children in the Worshipping Community, Ng and Thomas, Knox, 1981
Going to Church with Children, Stewart, JBCE, 1987
Children in the Church? Pedley & Muir, NS/CHP, 1997
Offering the Gospel to Children, Pritchard, Cowley/SPCK, 1992
Born Contemplative, Simon, DLT, 1993
Bringing Up Children in the Christian Faith, Westerhoff, Harper & Row, 1980
Building God's People, Westerhoff, Seabury Press, 1983

Worship in the home

The E Book, Ambrose, NS/CHP, 2000
Room for God, Evans, NS/CHP, 1996
A Story, a Hug and a Prayer, Foster, Kevin Mayhew, 1994
We Always Put a Candle in the Window, Freeman, NS/CHP, 1989
Prayers for Children, Herbert, NS/CHP, 1995
50 Family Activities, Ishmael, Kingsway, 2000
Family Fusion, Johnson, SU, 1991
Bumper Book of Family Activities, Marshall, SU, 1990

And All the Children Said Amen, Knox, SU, 1994
To Dance with God, Nelson, Paulist Press, 1986
Feast of Faith, Parkes, NS/CHP, 2000
Values Begin at Home, Ward, Victor Books, 1989

Initiation rites

Come & Join the Celebration, Muir & Pedley, NS/CHP, 2001
Children & Holy Communion, Pearce & Murrie, NS/CHP, 1997
Children & Communion—a Practical Guide, Reiss, Grove Booklet, 1998
Baptism Matters, Whitehead, NS/CHP, 1998
Welcome to the Lord's Table, Margaret Withers, BRF, 1999

All-age worship

All-Age Events & Worship, Castle, HarperCollins, 1994
All-Age Worship, Durran, Angel Press, 1987
Pick and Mix, Dean (ed.), NS/CHP, 1992
Signposts, Privett (ed.), NS/CHP, 1993
100 Instant Ideas for All-Age Worship, Relf, Kingsway Publications, 1998
Leaves on the Tree, ed. Jamal, NS/CHP, 1990
A Church for All Ages, Turner and Graystone, SU, 1993
Worship through the Christian Year, ed. Murrie & Bruce, NS/CHP, 1999
Wholly Worship, URC Publication, 2000

Material thematically linked to readings in the Revised Common Lectionary

Learning with the Sunday Gospels, Francis and Drayson, Mowbray
Vol 1: Advent to Pentecost 1998: Years A, B, C Worksheets, 1999
Vol 2: Trinity Sunday to Christ the King, 1999: Years A, B, C Worksheets, 2000
Living Stones, Sayers, Kevin Mayhew, 1997–99
Common Worship: Footsteps in Faith, Thompson, Kevin Mayhew, 1999
Common Worship: Step by Step, Thompson, Kevin Mayhew, 1999
Young Church Mag (puzzles/colouring sheets available through membership subscription from the Diocese of Exeter, Children's Work Department)
Worship through the Christian Year, NS/CPB, 1997–99

Children and spiritual gifts

Children Finding Faith, Bridger, SU/CPAS, 2000
Children & Evangelism, Frank, CPAS, 1992
Taking Children Seriously, Hubbard, Kingsway, 1991
Angels with Dirty Faces, Ishmael, Kingsway, 1989
Reclaiming a Generation, Ishmael Children's Ministry, 2001
And For Your Children, Leach, Monarch, 1994
Children and Renewal, Price, Hodder and Stoughton, 1996
Kingdom Kids, Sprange, Christian Focus, 1994

Using the Bible with children

Godly Play, Berryman, Augsberg, 1991
Teaching Godly Play, Berryman, Abingdon Press, 1995
Teaching the Bible to Children, Castle, Marshall Pickering, 1993
The Adventure Begins, Clutterham, Scripture Union/CPAS, 1996
Using the Bible With Children, Cox, Grove Booklet, 2000
The Bible, a Child's Playground, Gobbel & Gobbel, SCM Press, 1986
Readiness for Religion, Goldman, Seabury Press, 1970
Teaching Religion in School, Holm, OUP, 1975
Transforming Bible Study with Children, Van Ness, Abingdon Press, 1991
A Children's Guide to the Bible, Willoughby, Scripture Union, 1998

Bibles

Pre-schooler's Bible, Beers, Victor
The Toddler's Bible, Beers, Victor, 1992
The Lion Children's Bible, Lion Publishing, 1991
The Lion First Bible, Lion Publishing, 1997
The Beginners Bible, Kingsway, 1989 (for ages 3–8)
Holy Bible International Children's Bible, Word Bibles, 1991 (ages 7–11)
Contemporary English Version, Bible Society/HarperCollins, 1997
Kids Life Bible Storybook, Kingsway, 1994
The Beginner's Devotional, Kingsway, 1991

Leading children in prayer

Dreams and Visions, Fuller, Kevin Mayhew, 1997
Helping Children to Pray, Cardswell, The Grail, 1981
Prayers for Children, Herbert, NS/CHP, 1995
God Talk with Children, Hull, CEM, 1991
Praying with Children in the Home, Keiller, Grove Booklet No.42, 1992
101 Ideas for Creative Prayers, Merrell, Scripture Union, 1995
Dear God, Can You Wink? Raymond, Scripture Union, 1995
Children at Prayer, Stowe, Marshall Pickering, 1996

Growing a group

Strategic Church Leadership, Gill & Burke, SPCK, 1996
Raising the Standard, Harding, Kevin Mayhew, 1998
Teamwork, Jones, Scripture Union, 1995
Kaleidoscope Training Material, NCEC, 1993
Fired Up… Not Burnt Out, Withers, BRF, 2001
Power Pack Training Manual, Kevin Mayhew, 2000
Working with Children in the Church, NCEC, 1998

Age-specific guidelines

Children in Crèches, Croft, CPAS, 1995
Under 5s Welcome, Crawford, Scripture Union, 1990
Sharing Jesus with Under 5s, Gaukroger, Crossways Books, 1994
Working with Under 6s, Mullally, Scripture Union, 1997
Become Like a Child, Copsey, SU, 1994
Ten Plus, Baumohl, SU, 1984
The Art of 11–14s, CPAS/SU, 1996
Understanding Adolescence, Herding, Hodder & Stoughton, 1989
Time for Children—Tools for Reaching Under 12s, Clutterham (ed.), CPAS, 1996

A strategy for learning

Sunday Schools, Boylan, Yale University Press, 1988
Rise and Development of the Sunday School Movement, Cliff, NCEC, 1986
Learning Styles, LEFever, Kingsway, 1995
Learning & Teaching Together, Sutcliffe, Chester House Publications, 1980

Examples of curriculum materials for Christian nurture and worship

Under Construction, CPAS
Bible in Life learning materials, D.C. Cook
Living Stones, All-Age Revised Common Lectionary, Sayer, Kevin Mayhew, 1997
Whole People of God, Christian Education and Worship Lectionary, Canterbury Press
Partners in Learning, NCEC
Sharing and Learning Together SALT programme, Scripture Union
Children's Ministry Teaching Resources, Kingsway
Scripture Press materials
Feast Publications

Reaching children on the fringe

Creative Ideas for Youth Evangelism, Aiken, Marshall & Pickering, 1992
Children Finding Faith (2nd edition), Bridger, SU/CPAS, 2000
Outside In, Breen, Scripture Union, 1993
Reaching Families, Butler, Scripture Union, 1995
Kids Clubs, Clark & Pearson, Grove Booklets, 1999
Children and Evangelism, Frank, CPAS, 1992
Bringing Children to Faith, Frank, CPAS, 2000
Mission Possible, SU/CPAS, 2000
Building New Bridges, Gibbs, NS/CHP, 1996
Intergenerational Cell Resources, Kirk, Kevin Mayhew 1999
Early Harvest, Prince, Falcon, 1976
Whose is the Kingdom? Prince, Scripture Union, 1979
Working in Partnership with Schools, Watson, Grove Booklets, 1995
The Schools Workers' Handbook, Williams, Scripture Union, 1996

Reports

The Child in the Church, British Council of Churches, 1976
Understanding Christian Nurture, BCC, 1984
Communion before Confirmation? The Knaresborough Report, 1985
The Bible and Children, BCC, 1988
Children in the Way, NS/CHP, 1988
Children and Holy Communion, BCC, 1989
Working Together under the Children Act 1989, HMSO
All God's Children?, NS/CHP, 1991
Save our Children, A Response to All God's Children, Pearson, Grove Booklet, 1993
How Faith Grows, NS/CHP, 1991
Finding Faith Today, Finney, Bible Society, 1992
Children & The Bible, Report on 7–14s, Scripture Union, 1992
Unfinished Business, CCBI, 1994
Safe to Grow, Baptist Union, 1994
Safe From Harm, Home Office, HMSO, 1994
The Facts of Life, Barnardos, 1995
On the Way, CH/NS, 1995
Joining God's Church, Byworth, Reed & Waller, Grove Booklet, 1995
Something to Celebrate, NS/CHP, 1995
Family and Parenthood, Rowntree, 1995
Youth A Part, NS/CHP, 1996
Unfinished Business Reflection and Action, NCEC, 1997
The Tide is Running Out, English Church Survey, Peter Brierley, 2000

Agencies Working with Children and Young People

Denominationally based

Consultants and advisers are to be found across the denominations to help with work with children and young people. Contact can be made through diocesan offices, moderators and district superintendents.

Church Pastoral Aid Society
Athena Drive
Tachbrook Park
Warwick
CV34 6NG
Tel: 01926 334242
E-mail: mail@cpas.org.uk

CPAS has regional and national support networks and trains groups mainly in the Anglican Church. Provides a wide range of resources, including structured teaching programmes such as 'Under Construction'.

Crusaders
2 Romeland Hill
St Albans
AL3 4ET
Tel: 01727 855422
E-mail: crusaders@ukonline.co.uk

Non-uniform structured groups training and resources for church-based groups on a national and regional basis.

Children Worldwide
Dalesdown
Honeybridge Lane
Dial Post
Horsham
West Sussex
RH13 8NX
Tel: 01403 710712

Focus on serving the church through ministry to children and families by training leaders and leading children's events.

Children's Evangelism Ministry International
European & English Headquarters
6 Dock Offices
Surrey Quays Road
London
SE16 2XU
Tel: 020 7394 1677/020 7237 0404

Curbs Project
PO Box 344
Redhill
Surrey
RH1 3QQ
Tel: 01737 642522
E-mail: curbs.project@virgin.net

The Curbs project provides training and resources for children workers in the inner city and on outer estates.

Revd I Smale (Ishmael)
Revelation Centre
PO Box 38
Chichester
PO19 2UD
Website: www.ishmael.org.uk

A pioneer charismatic children's worker, especially in all-age worship.

Rural Sunrise
Sunrise Ministries
2 The Old Forge
Gardener Street
Hertsmonceaux
Hailsham
BN27 4LE
Tel: 01323 832083
E-mail: sunrise@ruralmissions.org.uk

Specialists in children's work in small and rural churches and schools.

Scripture Union
207–209 Queensway
Bletchley
Milton Keynes
Buckinghamshire
MK2 2EB
Tel: 01908 856000
E-mail: info@scriptureunion.org.uk

Scripture Union has field staff working in schools and church-based missions and holiday clubs, and can provide training.

Tecknon Trust
PO Box 239
Derby
DE22 1XH
Tel: 01332 372092
E-mail: club@tecknon.org

Offers a ministry of training for leaders and events for children with a charismatic focus.

Uniformed organizations providing resources group structures and training include:

Boys Brigade
Felden Lodge
Hemel Hempstead
Herts
HP3 0BL
Tel: 01422 235391

Girls Brigade
62 Foxhall Rd
Didcot
Oxfordshire
OX11 7BQ
Tel: 01235 510425

Campaigners
Campaigner House
St Mark's Close
Colney Heath
St Albans
Hertfordshire
AL4 ONQ
Tel: 01727 824065

Church Lads' & Church Girls' Brigade
2 Barnsley Road
Wath-upon-Dearne,
Rotherham
S63 6PY
Tel: 01709 876535

Publishers producing resources for children's work

BRF
First Floor
Elsfield Hall
15–17 Elsfield Way
Oxford
OX2 8FG
Tel: 01865 319700
E-mail: information@brf.org.uk

BRF produces training materials, Bible reading material and teaching resources, as well as offering training days, activity days and quiet days for adults and children up to the age of 11.

Church House Publishing
Tel: 0207 340 0276

Many books, especially focusing on church-based work.

Church Pastoral Aid Society

Books and training resources for all ages.

International Christian Communications
4 Regency Mews
Silverdale Rd
Eastbourne
East Sussex
BN20 7AB
Tel: 01323 643341

Publisher of tapes and books of the latest children's worship songs, including Spring Harvest range.

Kevin Mayhew
Tel: 01449 737978

A wide range, including guides and the popular *Instant Art* series.

Kingsway Publications
26–28 Lottbridge Drove
Eastbourne
East Sussex
BN23 GNT
Tel: 01323 410930
Website: www.childrensministry.co.uk

Books including all-age materials and talk outlines, as well as Children's Ministry training programme and *Children's Ministry* magazine.

Lion Publishing plc
Mayfield House
256 Banbury Road
Oxford
OX2 7DH
Tel: 01865 302750

Children's books including special seasonal activity books.

National Christian Education Council (NCEC) Partners in Learning
1020 Bristol Rd
Selly Oak
Birmingham
BS29 6LB
Tel: 0121 472 4242
E-mail: ncec@network.co.uk

Partners in Learning, an ecumenical resource for all ages linked to the Revised Common Lectionary.

Scripture Union

Books including the structured dated SALT material, Bible notes and holiday club outlines.

United Reformed Children's Information Network (Urchin)
URC House
86 Tavistock Place
London
WC1H 9RT

URCHIN termly magazine.

Mission agencies

CARE
53 Romney Street
London
SW1P 3RE
Tel: 020 7233 05455
E-mail: cfe@care.org.uk

Children's Society
Edward Rudolf House
London
WC1X 0JL
Tel: 020 7841 4400
E-mail: hq-reception@the-childrens-society.org.uk

Christian Aid
PO Box 100
London
SW1P 3RB
Tel: 020 7620 444
E-mail: caid@gn.apc.org

Cross Links
251 Lewisham Way
London
SE4 1XF
Tel: 020 8691 6111
E-mail: crosslinks@pro-net.co.uk

Chime Worldwide (Children in Mission & Evangelism)
11a Upper Teddington Road
Hampton Wick
Kingston-upon-Thames
KT1 4DL
Tel: 020 8977 5899

Church Mission Society (CMS)
Partnership House
157 Waterloo Rd
London
SE1 8XA
Tel: 020 7928 8681
E-mail: enquiries@cms.uk.org

Mothers' Union
Mary Summer House
24 Tufton Street
London
SW1P 3RB
Tel: 020 7222 5533
E-mail: mu@themothersunion.org

TEAR Fund
100 Church Rd
Teddington
Middlesex
TW11 8QE
Tel: 0845 355 8355
E-mail: enquiry@tearfund.org

Youth with a Mission (YWAM)
Highfield Oval
Ambrose Lane
Harpenden
AL5 4BX
Tel: 01582 765 481

United Society for the Propagation of the Gospel
Partnership House
157 Waterloo Rd
London
SE1 8XA
Tel: 020 7928 8681
E-mail: enquiries@uspg.org.uk

Viva Network
PO Box 633
Oxford
OX1 4YP
Tel: 01865 450800
E-mail: help@viva.org

Other useful agencies

CCPAS
PO Box 133
Swanley
Kent
BR8 7UQ
Tel: 0845 120 45 50
E-mail: info@ccpas.co.uk

An organization specializing in training, advice and counselling surrounding child safety and child abuse, helping churches and other organization to develop child protection plicies. In particular, CCPAS publish a training pack, 'Facing the Unthinkable', which will enable a church or group to provide a comprehensive in-house child protection training course. The pack comes with unlimited support and an updating service.

The National Society for the Prevention of Cruelty to Children (NSPCC) has local child protection teams and a 24-hour helpline, and can be contacted on 0800 800500.

Subject index

Abuse	14–15
Advocacy: raising child awareness	148–150
Affirmation	142, 161, 203
All-age worship	113–120
All God's Children report	15–16, 183
Aries, Philippe	53
Attachment relationship	60–62
Audits	151–152
Babies	57, 60, 71
Baptism	99
Berryman, Jerome	75, 137
Bible and leadership	163–164
Bible reading aids	111, 138
Bowlby, John	60–61
Bridger, Francis	84, 122
Budgets	150, 210–211
Celebrations	28, 192
Cavelletti, Sofia	79, 137
Characteristics of children	40, 81
Charismatic gifts and children	121–128
Charter for Children in the Church	103, 217–218
Childcare	61–63
Childhood and rights	25, 55
Childhood from a cultural perspective	54, 60
Childhood in the Old Testament	18–32
Child in the Church/Understanding Christian Nurture report	171
Childlessness	23, 26
Child protection	9, 149, 158
Children in a contemporary culture	10–15
Children in the Way report	15, 41, 43, 67, 82, 161, 172, 183
Children Learn What They Live (Nolte)	15
Children's Spirituality Project, University of Nottingham	81
Chrysostom	48
Church attendance	109, 185
Circumcision	22, 29
Clement	47
Cliff, Philip	170
Clutterham, Terry	129, 133–134
Coles, Robert	79–80
Commissioning service for leaders	160, 215–216
Consecration of firstborn	22–23
Conversion and children	187–188
Copsey, Kathryn	191
CURBS	191
Discipline	202–204
Divorce	13, 63–64
Donaldson, Margaret	75–76
Dunn, Judy	62–63
Early Christian writers	47–48
Early Church and children	44–51
Education	11, 28–30, 32, 50, 173–174
Enculturation	173, 175, 177
Engaging with the Bible	129–137
Environment	68–69
Evaluation	209–210, 213–214
Evangelism	182–193, 211
Faith development theories	79–82, 84–92
Family	13–14, 19–23, 33–36, 45–47, 60, 104–105, 178, 189–190
Fathers	24–25, 30, 63
Festivals as outreach	192
Fowler, James	85–87
Friendship	65, 67
Gobbel, Roger & Gobbel, Gertrude	132, 135
Godly Play	75, 137
Goldman, Ronald	73–75, 132–133
Good practice	143–144, 165
Grandparents	59, 63
Groome, Thomas	84, 131, 188
Hamilton, Bert	170
Hay, David & Nye, Rebecca	80
Health and safety	199–200
Hermeneutics	131
Historical perspectives and childhood	53–54
Holm, Jean	133
Holy Communion	94, 120
Holy Spirit	90, 97, 121–128, 136
How children think	71–77
Howkins, Ken	74
Hubbard, Richard	123, 126
Induction programme	160
Influences on children	11–15, 57–70
Ishmael (Ian Smale)	123, 126
Jesus and children	33–43
Job descriptions	158
Kidz Clubs	191–192
Language	76, 101, 110
Leach, John & Chris	125, 126
Leadership checklist	161

Leading children into prayer	139–146
Learning cycles	176
Learning strategy	175–181
Learning styles	176–177
London Bible College	42, 175, 194
Lone-parent families	13–14, 64
Media	12–13
Midweek clubs	190–192
Mission statements	195
New Directions in Children's Ministry	42, 175
Nixon, Rosemary	172
Nurturing children	30–32, 50, 99–100, 120, 171
Parent and toddler groups	212
Parenting in Old Testament community	23–25, 29–31
Partnership with school	192–193
Peer groups	91–92
Piaget, Jean	71–73, 77, 86, 132
Polycarp	47–48
Praying with children	144–145
Price, Alan	124–126, 128
Programme planning	179–181, 206–107
Reaching families in the community	189–190
Reaching wider contacts	190
Recruitment of leaders	156–167
Richards, Lawrence	26–17, 48
Robinson, Edward	75, 79
Shahar	54
'Simon Peter's journey of faith' exercise	91–92
Smith, Peter & Cowie, Helen	57
Social world of the child	59–70
Spirituality and faith	78–92
Sprange, Harry	123
Stages in social relationships	66
Strategy plans:	
All-age worship	117
Evangelism	186–193
Growing/developing a group	148–156
Learning	175–181
Recruiting/developing leaders	156–167
Worship in the home	107–112
Sunday schools	50, 169–175
Support of parents	107
Sutcliffe, John	172
Teamwork	157, 158
'Ten commandments for the place of children in church'	102–103
The Children Act 1989	25, 197, 199
Theological roots	17–51
The Tide is Running Out report	185–186
Tips for tired leaders	166–167
Training volunteers	156–157, 160
Unfinished Business report	16, 185
Uniformed organizations	190
Van Ness, Patricia	130, 134–135
Violence	14–15, 70
Vygotsky, Lev	77
Welcoming children in church	96, 99, 118
Westerhoff, John	85, 88–89, 95, 105, 108–109, 173–174, 177–178
What does leadership involve?	164–166
What makes a good leader?	161–163
Working agreements	159
Worship:	
A biblical pattern	106–107
Children's	39, 100–101
Definitions	94–95
In the covenant community	25–28
In the home	104–112
Theological basis for corporate worship	97–99
With children	101–103
Youth A Part report	16

Scripture index

Genesis 1:26	80	Deuteronomy 32:29	18
Genesis 1:28	20	Joshua 4:1–7	141
Genesis 4:1	21	Joshua 4:4–9	27
Genesis 12:1–3	22	Joshua 8:30–35	28
Genesis 12:2	20	Joshua 22:6–27	27
Genesis 15:5	22	Judges 6:15	19
Genesis 16:2	23	Ruth 4:11–12	20
Genesis 16:7–11	20	1 Samuel 1—3	27
Genesis 17:7	20	1 Samuel 1:5	23
Genesis 17:9	20	1 Samuel 1:11	21
Genesis 17:10–11	22	1 Samuel 1:23	28
Genesis 17:12–13	22	1 Samuel 2:12—3:18	25
Genesis 17:14	22	1 Samuel 2:18	26
Genesis 17:20–23	29	1 Samuel 3:1–21	141
Genesis 17:23–27	29	1 Samuel 3	79
Genesis 19:30–38	21	1 Samuel 9:17–21	19
Genesis 20:18	23	2 Kings 4:1	24
Genesis 24:60	20	2 Kings 5:1–3	79
Genesis 26:4	20	2 Kings 11:21	79
Genesis 30:1–9	23	1 Chronicles 1—9	19
Genesis 42:37	24	2 Chronicles 20:1–19	28
Exodus 3:5–6	73	Nehemiah 5:5	24
Exodus 4:24–26	22	Nehemiah 8:1–3	141
Exodus 12:21–27	141	Nehemiah 8:5–12	141
Exodus 12:25–27	27	Nehemiah 8:10	170
Exodus 12:43	22	Psalm 8:2	24, 79
Exodus 13:2	22	Psalm 78:1–4	106
Exodus 20	20	Psalm 78:1–6	8
Exodus 21:7	24	Psalm 78:3–6	29
Exodus 22:21–24	23	Psalm 88:3–9	20
Leviticus 16:29–34	141	Psalm 107:1–3	166
Deuteronomy 1:39	24	Psalm 107:5–7	166
Deuteronomy 4:1	31	Psalm 107:8–9	167
Deuteronomy 4:1–10	30	Psalm 107:9	168
Deuteronomy 4:9–10	106	Psalm 148:12	18
Deuteronomy 4:9	170	Psalm 148:11–12	24
Deuteronomy 4:25–26	106	Proverbs 22:6	181
Deuteronomy 4:37–40	106	Ecclesiastes 12:1	26
Deuteronomy 6:1–9	30	Isaiah 1:17	23
Deuteronomy 6:4–7	106	Isaiah 7:14–16	24
Deuteronomy 6:6–7	99	Isaiah 33:22	29
Deuteronomy 6:20–21	30	Isaiah 49:19–23	167
Deuteronomy 6:20–25	141	Isaiah 50:1	24
Deuteronomy 10:18	23	Jeremiah 1:1	19
Deuteronomy 12:1–32	28	Jeremiah 7:18ff.	170
Deuteronomy 21:16–17	22	Ezekiel 9:6	18
Deuteronomy 25:5–10	21	Hosea 14:3	23
Deuteronomy 32:25	18	Matthew 4:8ff.	91

Matthew 7:9–10	179
Matthew 11:16–19	39
Matthew 11:25	79
Matthew 12:46	35
Matthew 13:31–32	133
Matthew 14:13–21	170
Matthew 18:1–5	34
Matthew 18:2–5	42
Matthew 18:3–4	41
Matthew 18:6	187
Matthew 18:6–7	41
Matthew 19:13–14	33
Matthew 19:13–15	42, 170
Matthew 21:15–17	39
Matthew 21:12–16	25
Matthew 21:16	79
Matthew 28:19–20a	128
Mark 2:13–17	186
Mark 5:21–24	38
Mark 5:35–43	38
Mark 7:25–30	38
Mark 9:14–27	39
Mark 9:33–37	34
Mark 9:37	40
Mark 10:13–15	98
Mark 10:13–16	33, 40, 170
Mark 10:17–23	186
Luke 1:36	35
Luke 2:40	34
Luke 2:41–52	36
Luke 2:52	34
Luke 7:31–35	39
Luke 9	91
Luke 10:21	38
Luke 15	179
Luke 17:11–19	180
Luke 18:15–17	170
John 3:3–8	122
John 4	186
John 4:24	122
John 4:46–53	39
John 6:1–15	38
John 8	186
John 14:16	122
John 16:8	122
John 18:15–18	92
John 18:25–27	92
John 19:25–27	35
John 21	92
Acts 1:8	122
Acts 2—4	91
Acts 2:39	122
Acts 2:42–47	49
Acts 10	92
Acts 17:32–34	186
Romans 8:15–17	122
Romans 8:26	122
Romans 12	165
Romans 12:6–8	49
Romans 13:9–16	49
Romans 15:14	49
Romans 16:5	49
1 Corinthians 12:7–11	49
1 Corinthians 12:12–13	98
1 Corinthians 12:27–30	121
1 Corinthians 13:1–3	128
1 Corinthians 13:11	71, 83
1 Corinthians 14:26	49
1 Corinthians 14:29–31	49
2 Corinthians 4:3–4	186
Galatians 3:23–25	18
Galatians 3:26–28	122
Galatians 4:4–5	37
Ephesians 3:14–21	142
Ephesians 4:11–13	49
Ephesians 4:15–16	99
Ephesians 6:1	46
Ephesians 6:1–4	45, 107
Ephesians 6:4	46
Ephesians 6:18–19	140
Philippians 2:6–11	42
Philippians 4:6	140
Colossians 3:11	98
Colossians 3:20	46
Colossians 3:20–21	107
Colossians 3:20–23	45
Colossians 3:21	46
Colossians 4:2	140
1 Thessalonians 5:16–18	140
1 Thessalonians 5:24	164
1 Timothy 2:1–2	140
1 Timothy 3:4–5	46, 107
1 Timothy 4:1–16	163
2 Timothy 1:5	51
2 Timothy 3:12	50
2 Timothy 3:14	50–51
2 Timothy 3:15	51
Hebrews 2:17–18	36
Hebrews 10:23–26	49
James 5:13–14	140
1 Peter 2:2	84, 92
2 Peter 3:3–8	92